Hut Hopping in the Austrian Alps

A Sierra Club Totebook™
by William E. Reifsnyder

San Francisco • New York

The Sierra Club, founded in 1892 by John Muir, has devoted itself to the study and protection of the nation's scenic and ecological resources — mountains, wetlands, woodlands, wild shores and rivers. All club publications are part of the nonprofit effort the club carries on as a public trust. There are more than 42 chapters coast to coast, in Canada, Hawaii and Alaska. Participation is invited in the club's program to enjoy and preserve wilderness everywhere. Address: 1050 Mills Tower, San Francisco, California 94104; 597 5th Avenue, New York, N.Y. 10017, or 324 C Street, S.E., Washington, D.C. 20003

Photographs by William E. Reifsnyder.
Library of Congress catalog card number 73-77290.
International Standard Book number 87156-081-X.
Produced in New York by Harold Black Inc., and printed in the United States of America by Fred Weidner & Son Printers, Inc.

I. Tips

II. Trips

Introduction

Conjure the Alps: vast fields of ice and snow, separated by towering peaks with sheer walls, accessible only by experienced rock climbers; untracked vastnesses where only a native guide can find his way; a strange land inhabited mainly by mountain goats and people who speak strange tongues; in sum, a place where only the most intrepid and adventuresome would dare to venture. Right?

Wrong. The Alps are as accessible as the White Mountains of New Hampshire; more accessible than the Sierra Nevada of California. They come in all sizes and shapes, from gentle, fir-covered foothills to vertical rock faces, with all the variations in between. They are covered with an intricate network of marked and graded trails, some easy, some challenging. And the Austrian Alps in particular are served by a network of mountain hostels, the *Schutzhütte* operated by the Alpine clubs and others, which provide food, shelter and camaraderie for Alpine hikers.

Of course, the Alps do offer some of the most challenging rock- and ice-climbing opportunities in the world, and not only on the north face of the

Eiger or the sheer rock slopes of the Matterhorn. The rock-climber nevertheless is outnumbered ten-to-one by hikers like you and me, who find their greatest joy in just being in the high mountains, happy with their home on their backs, exultant with the sense of well-being that permeates them as they stride along a mountain path, breathing deeply of the clear air with nothing but beauty and grandeur to meet the eyes. The Alps are full of hikers: the mountain-loving Austrians and Germans and the Swiss, the French, the Dutch, the English. But where are the Americans? Americans have invaded the towns and cities, the autobahns and the railroads. But they are strangely absent in the mountains. I have been in mountain huts where, so far as I could tell from the register, I was the first American visitor.

In the pages that follow, I hope to stimulate your interest in hiking in the Alps, to the extent that you may actively plan such a trip and tote this book along to aid you on the trail. It *is* easy, and it is becoming easier and less expensive all the time with trans-Atlantic air fares tumbling. All of the information you will need to take such a trip is here: where to go, how to get there, what to take, detailed trail descriptions for three tours. The hikes are graded in strenuousness from easy to moderately difficult. All are in spectacular portions of the Austrian Alps. And they are designed to utilize the ubiquitous Alpine Hut, so that you will have no need to carry sleeping gear or large quantities of food. Anyone who has hiked or backpacked in any of the mountains of North America will find himself at home on these trips.

The huts are one of the great joys of Alpine hiking in Austria. There are more than five hundred of them, all open to the public, providing meals and sleeping accommodations at very reasonable prices. Because of them, hiking in the Alps is quite a different experience from hiking in America. Tenting and bivouacking are almost unknown in the Alps; nearly everyone overnights in the huts. Whereas in the Sierra of California, for example, nighttime will find parties spread out over the landscape, in the Alps all will be concentrated in the huts. In the morning, hikers and climbers fan out from the hut, ascending a nearby peak, or traversing a pass to the next hut. But at night they will always stay at a hut.

There is an important ecological lesson here. Even though Alpine trails receive very heavy use, the impact of the hiker is minimal. He does not pitch a tent, build a fireplace, gather wood, trample the earth around his campsite, leave his debris. He merely passes by, and the only sign of his passage is his spoor. The impact is concentrated at the huts, where it can be dealt with adequately. As a result, although many parts of the Alps are more heavily used than sections of the Sierra, the visible impact of man's recreational use is less.

This is not to say that there are no problems of overuse and misuse in the Alps. I have seen unsightly garbage dumps next to some of the huts; I have even seen debris dumped into a nearby stream. Gum wrappers are ubiquitous. In earlier times, when food came in reusable bottles and jars, or was wrapped in paper, the amount of "hard" garbage was almost nil. But today, even though in central Europe most drinks are still bottled in reusable containers, there is a growing quantity of nonreusable bottles, cans, and plastic containers of one sort or another. And this is beginning to present problems not only at the huts, but also along the trails, especially at concentration points such as mountain summits.

Still, there is an ecological lesson. Maintaining the semblance of a pristine wilderness, an ecological balance that is close to "natural" in the face of heavy recreational use by hikers, requires the kind of intensive management that has developed in the Alps. That is, the damaging aspects of use — those connected with "housekeeping" activities — *must* be concentrated in areas where the impact can be minimized by appropriate management. This can be accomplished by concentrating such use in mountain inns as is done in the Alps and in the huts of the Appalachian Mountain Club in the

White Mountains of New Hampshire, or it can be
done by limiting camping to carefully prepared and
outfitted campsites, as in the Boundary Waters
Canoe Area in Minnesota. But it is clear that unreg-
ulated use by large numbers of people, no matter
how sensitive they are to wilderness values, can
only result in heavy impacts and destruction of the
wilderness.

But to get back to the subject of the book,
which is an invitation to sample the delights of
hut-hopping in the Austrian Alps. The pages that
follow will tell you in considerable detail how to
get to the Alps and what to do when you get there.
The information is predicated on the assumption
that you have some experience in hiking and/or
backpacking in the United States. It is therefore
not a complete exposition of the intricacies of
backpacking. A book such as Colin Fletcher's *The
Complete Walker* is recommended for that. This
work also assumes that you have never been to
Europe before, do not speak German (the language
of the Austrian Alps) and that you are not familiar
with travel customs, eating habits and so forth.
Those who have traveled in Europe may find some
of the information quite unnecessary. But I remember my first trip to Germany, when I was
dumped off the airplane at Frankfurt and had to
find my way to Wolfsburg, with only the most
elementary knowledge of the German language,

and none whatsoever on how to purchase a railroad ticket. The first trip, however, need not be difficult. Armed with the suggestions that follow, you will have little difficulty in finding your way to and through the mountains.

And believe me, it is worth it! Hut-hopping in the Austrian Alps is a joyous experience: trails stretching from pass to pass, clinging to high slopes above timberline where every step brings a new and spectacular view. Clear mountain streams, Alpine flowers in profusion, the flash of a mountain goat bounding over steep talus. And at the end of a strenuous day's walking, the comfort and camaraderie of the Alpine hut, good food, good drink, and a comfortable bed in which to dream of the next day's adventures. Come, join me in a week's walking tour along the high trails of the Austrian Alps . . . .

I. Tips

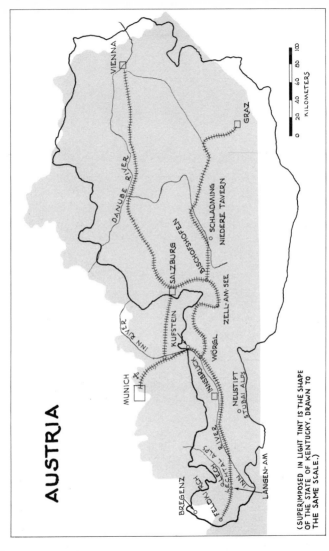

AUSTRIA

MUNICH

BREGENZ
FELDKIRCH
LECHTAL ALPS
LANGEN-AM
INN RIVER

INNSBRUCK
WÖRGL
KUFSTEIN
NEUSTIFT
STUBAI ALPS

SALZBURG
BISCHOFSHOFEN
ZELL-AM-SEE
SCHLADMING
NIEDERE TAVERN

VIENNA

DANUBE RIVER
INN RIVER

GRAZ

(SUPERIMPOSED IN LIGHT TINT IS THE SHAPE
OF THE STATE OF KENTUCKY, DRAWN TO
THE SAME SCALE.)

0   20   40   60   80   100
KILOMETERS

Austria (Kentucky outlined at same scale).

1. The setting: topography, geology, climate and vegetation

The Austrian Alps, the so-called Eastern Alps, stretch in an east-west band about 300 miles from Vienna in the east to the Swiss border in the west. They continue westward through Switzerland, then arc sharply southwestward along the French-Italian border. The western neck of Austria is dominated by the mountains; only in eastern Austria does the landscape flatten out.

Austria is remarkably similar in size, shape and orientation to the state of Kentucky (see map). Kentucky is slightly larger, about 39,000 square miles, compared to 34,000 for Austria. Here the comparison ends. Austria is 10 degrees farther north, at 47°N, the latitude of Seattle and northern Maine. Everything else is different, too: topography, geology, climate, vegetation.

The highest peak in the Eastern Alps is the Gross Glockner at 12,641 feet above sea level (the highest in Europe: Mont Blanc, at 15,782 feet). There are hundreds of peaks over 10,000 feet.

Geologically, the Alps were formed by crumpling pressures from north and south that caused great sheets of rock to fold and slide over one another. The crumpling resulted in a series of east-west ridges and mountain chains separated by long valleys. For example, the Inn River, on which Innsbruck is located, flows east-northeastward through western Austria to the German border where it turns northward to flow across the Bavarian plain to the Danube. Tributary valleys generally trend north-south. The passes on the south, such as the Brenner (4,495 feet), lead to Italy. To the north of the mountains, in Germany, lies a great outwash plain formed by the retreating Pleistocene glaciers. The mountains forming the northern boundary of the Alps are breached in several places by major rivers. The Inn River cuts through the Bavarian Alps at an elevation of 1,500 feet.

This northern mountain chain is composed pri-

Terminal moraines left by receding glacier.

marily of calcareous rocks. The mountains around Lech, described subsequently, are near the western end of this band. To the south, the mountains are generally crystalline in nature, primarily schists and gneisses. The described tours in the Stubai and in the Schladminger Tauern are in this region. Farther south lies another band of calcareous rocks, the Dolomites of Italy.

The Alps were heavily glaciated during the Pleistocene, and the many glaciers existing today are remnants of this period. Although the longest Alpine glacier is in Switzerland (the Aletsch, 16 miles long), portions of the Austrian Alps are liberally endowed with glaciers. The Pasterz glacier, on the slopes of the Gross Glockner, is six miles long. During the Pleistocene, only the highest peaks stood above the ice mass, and evidence of glacial activity is to be seen everywhere.

Because they were formed in recent geologic time, Alpine slopes are precipitous. This is as true of the Eastern Alps as it is of their higher neighbors to the west in Switzerland. Pleistocene glaciation produced many hanging valleys similar to those opening into Yosemite Valley in the Sierra of California, and many of the Alpine huts are located at the ends of these valleys. This has had an important consequence for the development and operation of the huts. Although generally inaccessible by road, many huts are visible, or nearly so, from the roadhead in the lower valley. Cableways have been constructed to the huts from the valleys below, and have thus permitted easy transport of goods and construction materials. But the trails to the huts are often steep and climb two or three thousand feet, switchbacking past spectacular waterfalls.

Climate

It is often said that mountains make their own climate, and the Alps are no exception. Because the mountains are oriented east-west across Europe, they permit the flow of moist maritime air from the Atlantic Ocean deep into the continent. Thus, the climate is wetter and warmer than might be expected for such latitudes.

The east-west trend of the mountains accentuates latitudinal variations: the southern slopes of the Alps, though at the latitude of Mont Tremblant in Quebec, have a climate that is much closer to that of the southern Sierra Nevada in California, ten degrees farther south.

The weather of the main mountain chain is dominated by storms from the Atlantic interrupted by periods of high pressure with generally clear and dry conditions. These storms occur in summer as well as in winter (though less frequently in summer).

Precipitation is more or less uniformly distribut-

Cable car hauling supplies.

ed throughout the year. Amounts vary greatly, depending on altitude. Innsbruck, at an elevation of 1,970 feet (580 m.) has an annual precipitation of 36 inches, of which 40 percent falls during the months of June, July and August. July is the rainiest single month. Precipitation increases markedly with altitude, and the climatic station on the Patscherkofel, just above Innsbruck at an elevation of 6,000 feet (1,830 m.) has an annual total of 47 inches.

Lightning and thunderstorms are frequent in the mountains, especially in early summer. At Innsbruck, the average number of days with a thunderstorm is 5.3 in June, 7.4 in July, 4.9 in August, and 1.8 in September. Some rain can be expected in these four months on 21, 22, 20 and 16 days, respectively. Although summer precipitation is always in the form of rain in the lower valleys, as at Innsbruck, it may be snow at higher elevations. I vividly remember being snowed in for two days at the Biberacher Hut near Lech (elevation: 6,055 feet, or 1846 m.) during a late August storm that put nearly two feet of snow on the ground. Snowstorms are rare at such low elevations in summer; but above about 8,000 feet snow may fall any time.

Temperatures in the Alps are influenced by topography and elevation. Average temperatures decrease by about three degrees for every thousand feet of elevation. Thus, while the yearly average temperature is 47°F at Innsbruck, on the summit of the Zugspitze, 20 miles away and 8,000 feet higher, it is 23°F or 24 degrees colder. Topographic configuration also exerts a tremendous influence on temperature, especially in the daily range. Valleys and basins in which cold air can collect at night, and which are protected from daytime winds, have much greater daily ranges than nearby mountain peaks and ridges. For example, in one set of observations comparing a valley station at 1,600 feet with a nearby mountaintop station at 5,800 feet, early morning temperatures (at 0730) in July averaged 60°F and 49°F, respectively. The comparable afternoon temperatures (at 1330) were 71°F and 53°F. Thus the average difference in the valley was 11 degrees while on the mountaintop it was only four degrees.

In deep valleys within the mountains, the shading effect of nearby ridges can have tremendous influence on temperatures and human comfort. Many huts are at the bottoms of such valleys and may receive little direct sunshine during the day, especially late in the summer near the autumnal equinox. At the latitude of Innsbruck, the noon sun on June 21 is only 43° above the horizon. Any north-facing slope greater than this angle will not receive any sun at all at this time of year.

Since Austria is so far north, days are long in

early summer — at the solstice, nearly 16 hours from sunrise to sunset. This, together with the higher altitude of the sun, means that 50 percent more energy is received by the earth's surface in early summer than in September. Table I gives

Table I

Time of sunrise, sunset, solar noon and daylength
Times are local standard time at Innsbruck, Austria

Date	Sunrise	Sunset	Daylength hr:min	Solar noon	Solar altitude at noon degrees
30 May	0423	2000	15:37	1212	64
10 June	0418	2009	15:51	1214	65
20 June	0418	2014	15:56	1216	66
30 June	0422	2014	15:53	1218	65
10 July	0429	2010	15:41	1220	64
20 July	0439	2002	15:24	1221	63
30 July	0451	1951	15:00	1221	60
10 August	0505	1935	14:30	1220	57
20 August	0518	1918	14:00	1218	54
30 August	0531	1859	13:28	1215	50
10 September	0545	1837	12:52	1211	46
20 September	0559	1817	12:18	1208	42
30 September	0612	1756	11:44	1204	38

Note: For Lech, times will be about five minutes later than those in table; for Schladming, times will be about nine minutes earlier; for Stubai, times are correct.

Timberline in the Schladminger Tauern.

times of sunrise, sunset and solar noon, together with daylength and the altitude of the sun at noon, for Innsbruck. The table is useful for planning hiking times, especially for long stretches.

Vegetation

Timberline in the Austrian Alps lies near the 6,000-foot contour, as in the White Mountains of New Hampshire, while the snow line is generally 1,000 feet higher. In this upper zone, there are extensive pastures, or *alms*, which are used for grazing cattle and sheep in the summer months. Indeed, there is considerable evidence that the natural tree line has been lowered about 600 feet because of the heavy grazing. It has even been suggested that much of the avalanche damage in the Alps can be traced to this deforestation, for the lowered tree line is now the principal starting zone for snow avalanches.

Alpine flora above timberline is rich and varied; more than 700 species have been recorded. Because of heavy human and animal use of this zone, and because of the fragility of the flora, many plants are protected by law. Although the list varies from region to region, it is well-publicized by color posters showing the protected plants. Picking some plants, such as Edelweis, is completely forbidden. With others, it is permissible to pick one or two for purposes of a collection. The Alpine huts usually have the protected flower poster displayed in a prominent place. (Flower buffs can find a number of pocket guides in the bookstores. They are mostly in German, but translating the flower names is generally easy and obvious.)

The characteristic timberline trees are Arolla pine (*Pinus cembra*) and mountain pine (*P. mugo*). Below this zone, Norway spruce (*Picea abies*) is the dominant species, and it forms extensive pure stands, many of which have been planted. Larch, silver fir and Scotch pine are also found in this zone. Below about 4,000 feet, conifers give way to mixed hardwoods, with beech, oak, ash and sycamore predominating.

The general impression provoked by Alpine

geography is one of great openness. Rarely does the hiker walk through great stretches of dense forest. Nearly always one can see where he is going and from whence he came. The vegetational pattern is largely dominated by man's influence, except, of course, in the high Alpine zone. In the valleys, much of the land has been cleared for agriculture, and the forests that remain are in small patches. Even on the steeper slopes above the agricultural zone, much of the forest was long ago converted to grazing land and has been maintained in that condition for so many years that the landscape appears perfectly natural. In appearance, there is no region of the United States that is comparable, although superficially many of the mountains of the western States appear somewhat similar. There, however, the tree cover tends to be sparse for lack of moisture, not man's cultural activities.

Fauna

It sometimes seems that the only animals left in the Alps are the cow, the sheep and the goat. The tinkle of the sheep bell and the deeper clank of the cowbell can be heard almost anywhere. Above timberline, one may occasionally see chamois, a relative of the antelope. (I actually saw a pair on the slopes of the Hochgolling in the Schladminger Tauern.) Deer are common in lower elevations in the forest, but are hard to spot. Marmots are common at very high elevations near the snow line, and one may occasionally see mice and chipmunks.

Birds are numerous, even at very high elevations. Again, good pocket guides are readily available in bookstores. Insects, especially those pesty to man, are not common, although butterflies may be seen above timberline, and indeed are an important agent of pollination of many Alpine plants. Poisonous snakes are not present in the Alps.

Cultural geography

The dominant impression one has of the Austrian

Schröcken, high in the Lechtaler Alps.

Alps is that man is and has been everywhere. Every valley that permits the construction of a road or track is inhabited. In the narrow valleys, the *Strassendorf* (literally, street village) is common; buildings and farmhouses straggle along a road that winds deep into the mountains. Where more space is available, one encounters the *Haufendorf*: a small cluster of houses and barns. But the isolated farmhouse, the *Einzelhof*, is also to be seen in the valleys and on the lower slopes of the mountains. At high elevations, the *Almhütte*, a small log or stone hut, provides summer dwelling for the villagers who move up to tend cattle. Small barns and hay storage sheds are also common above timberline.

For the hiker, the cultural density can be both good and bad. It is almost impossible to get away from the sights of civilization. Nearly every vista includes a valley in which a farmhouse or village can be seen. But what is lost in terms of wilderness experience is gained in accessibility. Few places cannot be reached in a day's walk from the nearest roadhead; and as indicated in the chapter on transportation, most of the roads have some sort of public transport, whether train, bus, jeep or taxi. And numerous chair lifts and gondolas stretch upward from the larger villages, providing access to the higher elevations.

2. Transportation and accommodations

One of the things that makes a trip to the Alps so attractive is the ease of getting there. It is also inexpensive, and if the airlines cut transatlantic fares to match the non-skeds, transportation will be plentiful and cheap. For a New Yorker, it can be cheaper to spend three weeks hiking in the Alps than to make a similar trip to the Sierra Nevada in California.

The Austrian Alps may be approached via either Munich or Zurich. Both have excellent air service from the United States and Canada. And both have excellent rail service to the heart of the Alps. Trans World Airlines and Swissair serve Zurich, while Pan Am and Lufthansa fly to Munich. Service to both may also be available through group tours, either on one of the scheduled airlines, or on one of the non-scheduled air carriers. You should check with a travel agency to find out possibilities for group tour rates, and for special tourist rates offered by the airlines. Students often may take advantage of group fares arranged through campus organizations, often at fantastically low prices.

The western end of the Austrian Alps, the area around Lech described in Chapter 8, is most easily reached from Zurich. There is direct train service to Innsbruck via Langen am Arlberg, the gateway to the Lechtaler Alps. The Zurich Airport (*Flughafen*) is ten kilometers (six miles) due north of the center of the city. Frequent bus service is available from the airport to the main railroad station (*Hauptbahnhof*), and there are hotels of all sorts nearby. The Zurich Tourist Office (*Verkehrsverein Zürich*) is near the entrance to the railroad station, on the *Bahnhof-Platz*, and the clerks are helpful in finding overnight hotel accommodations.

For the central and eastern regions, Munich is the natural gateway. (Innsbruck is two hours from Munich by train: Langen am Arlberg is two hours from Innsbruck, with a change of trains there. Langen am Arlberg is three hours from Zurich, with Innsbruck another two hours away on the same train.)

Arrival in Munich is at the Munich-Riem Airport, a few miles east of the city. Buses marked *Hauptbahnhof* (main railroad station) may be boarded right at the main entrance of the air terminal, and leave for downtown frequently. The fare is 2½ marks, approximately 75 cents.

The Hauptbahnhof is in the heart of downtown Munich. It is really three stations in one, the main station being flanked on the south by the Holzkirchner station and on the north by the Starnberger station. The airport buses terminate at the north side of the main station.

Travel by rail in central Europe is so easy, comfortable and inexpensive that it is a wonder there are so many cars on the road. For the hiker, an auto is a drag, for he is always tied to it. Reliance on public transportation permits much greater flexibility in choosing the starting and ending points for high-country trips. Austria has an extensive rail network, and where the railroads don't go, a bus line almost certainly does. Taxis and jeeps are common, too, but more about them later.

Railroad stations have large timetables posted in prominent locations, and the Munich *Hauptbahnhof* is no exception. These large signs indicate the arrivals (*Ankunft*) and departures (*Abfahrt*) in time sequence, and include information on the track number (*Gleis*). Tickets are purchased at the *Fahrkartenschalter*. For short trips, there is no point in traveling any other way than by second class (*Zweite Klasse*), which is considerably cheaper than first class and no less comfortable and clean.

Trains are classified according to speed and number of stops, much as in the U.S. The *Personenzug* is the local train, and base fares are usually given for this slower train. The *Expresszug* (abbreviated *Ex*) and the *Eilzug* (*E*) make fewer stops, and the *Schnellzug* (abbreviated *D*) is the fastest of all. One special train you may see is the TEE, the *Trans-Europ-Express*. Fares on the last two trains, the D and TEE, carry a premium called a *Zuschlag*. For the trip to Innsbruck or Salzburg, there are a number of the fast trains. On these, the time to Innsbruck is just over two hours; to Salzburg, about an hour and a half. Incidentally, the fastest route to Innsbruck is via Kufstein. Another route goes through Garmisch-Partenkirchen, which though shorter in distance, winds through the mountains and takes about a half hour longer.

A round-trip ticket from Munich to Innsbruck on the D-Zug, second class accommodations, would be described to the ticket-seller as follows: *"Eine Fahrkarte, bitte, Innsbruck hin und zurück, zweite Klasse, mit Schnellzug Zuschlag."* One-way tickets are known as *"Einfach,"* i.e., single or simple tickets.

There is scarcely a town or village in Austria that does not have regularly scheduled transportation, especially in the summer season. Many of these are operated by the *Osterreichischer Bundesbahn*, the Austrian state railroad, but some are run by local towns or private agencies. Timetables and prices for the national railroad and bus system are contained in the *Excelsior Taschenfahrplan*, obtainable at the Innsbruck station for about 50 cents. It is a good investment, for it also contains timetables for the Innsbruck streetcar and bus lines, as well as the numerous buslines running out from Innsbruck to various towns in the nearby area.

And where buses fail to run, taxis are sure to go. In small rural railroad stations, the stationmaster will usually be obliging enough to call the taxi for you. A further convenience in reaching the beginning of the trail is the existence of "jeep" lines that run from the ends of the bus lines up the valleys over the gravel roads as far as they are passable. Most of these services utilize four-wheel-drive Land Rovers and are run especially for hikers and climbers. Specific availability of these is indicated in the chapters describing the trail trips.

A word about hitch-hiking in Austria: Don't. There simply is no tradition for this most inexpensive way of getting around. I have never tried it myself, but I have talked to many young American students who have, and their universal experience has been bad. They wait for hours, even days sometimes, before catching a ride.

Information

Travel information is very easy to come by in the main tourist areas of central Europe. Every major railroad station has its *Auskunft* window or office. Attendants often speak English, but it is common courtesy to speak slowly and distinctly when you are expecting someone else to understand a language that is not his own. Your attempts to speak German will be appreciated, and will usually elicit a response in English (at least if your German is as bad and Anglicized as mine).

Every tourist town — and that includes just about *every* town in Austria — publishes informational brochures. These are often available at the railroad station or at the *Touristenverkehrsbüro*, the tourist office in town. The *Wohnungsnachweis* (dwelling plan or map) contains a list and map of every house and hotel in the village, with information on type and number of accommodations. These lists of hotels and guest houses (*Gasthöfe* or *Gaststätten*) also give the room prices, telephone numbers and other data.

Larger cities such as Innsbruck and Munich publish more elaborate maps and brochures, frequently containing suggestions of things to do and see. It is perhaps too easy to accumulate a great quantity of these informational brochures, but they can be very helpful in finding a place to stay in a strange town.

There are numerous English-language tourist guidebooks available for Austria; American bookstores are full of them just before the tourist season. One of the best is the Michelin *Green Guide to Austria and the Bavarian Alps*. It is published in an English edition by The Dickens Press in London, but is generally available in the U.S. The *Green Guide* is oriented toward the auto tourist and has good maps, both regional and local. It also has city maps for many Austrian cities.

The major oil companies publish good road maps that may be purchased at gas stations. (Many things are inexpensive in Europe; few things are free).

Few towns or cities in Europe are without a camping area. These are generally well-run commercial establishments, some with nearly all of the comforts of home: hot showers, flush toilets, restaurants. But the camping area itself is usually a large field, devoid of trees, tables and fireplaces. So, bring at least something to cook on and something to eat from, and, of course, a tent. Charges are nominal. Many road maps show *Campingplatz* locations, but guidebooks are available. A good one is the *Internationaler Camping Führer*, published by the ADAC (the German Auto Club) in Munich, and available in most bookstores. Vol. 1 covers Germany and north Europe; Vol. 2 covers Austria and Switzerland and south Europe.

Accommodations in town

Because Austria is so tourist-oriented, nearly every householder seems to have at least one room to rent. The *Zimmer frei* sign is everywhere. Rooms are not free, as the sign might indicate, but they are inexpensive. A typical price for a single-bed room in a *Pension* or small hotel is two dollars, and invariably includes *Frühstück*, the continental breakfast consisting of coffee, bread or rolls and butter and jam. Less expensive accommodations may be had, and even the larger hotels are not much more (except, of course, the fancy "American" hotels).

For the economy-minded student and young adult, Austria and Germany have a wide network of youth hostels. They are very inexpensive, offering beds for about 50 cents, but you must bring your own sheet sleeping sack. Some of the hostels in the larger cities are large establishments, run like hotels. They are a good bet for the hiker on a minimum budget, and offer comfortable clean accommodations at a minimum price. Information on joining the American Youth Hostels, which qualifies one to use the European hostels, may be obtained from the main U.S. headquarters at 20 West 17th Street, New York, New York, 10011. A guidebook and map showing the locations of hostels may be obtained from the AYH office for $2.60.

Incidentally, a room with bath is very rare and very expensive in Austria. A hot bath in a pension can cost half as much as the room itself. And soap is *never* provided; bring your own.

Accommodations in Innsbruck

As might be expected, accommodations in Innsbruck are more expensive and somewhat harder to find than in the smaller towns in the countryside.

There are, of course, good hotels downtown near the railroad station, but they tend to cater to the "wealthy American tourist" and furthermore may be full during the tourist season. There is, however, a 200-bed youth hostel in Innsbruck (on Gabelsbergerstrasse, near the railroad station), and any number of small and relatively inexpensive pensions. One place I found to be very satisfactory is the Student Hotel (*Studentenheim*) at the University of Innsbruck. During the winter, it serves as a dormitory for students; in the summer it is run as a hotel, open to the general public. Although it is about a mile from the railroad station (on *Josef-Hirn Strasse*, near University Bridge), it is a good, clean, informal and inexpensive place to stay. Although a single room costs about four dollars, breakfast is included and the showers are free.

Travel documents

You will, of course, need a passport. Many post-offices in the U.S. now have passport offices, where application may be made. Apply several months in advance; although the process has been speeded up in recent years, nothing is quite so unnerving as wondering which will arrive first—your passport or your departure date. While you are obtaining the necessary passport photos, have several extras made to take with you. If you join the *Alpenverein*, for example, you will need two passport-sized photos. Although coin-operated photo booths can be found in the large European cities, they are not to be trusted.

Take along your immunization record. Requirements have eased much; the U.S. no longer requires a smallpox vaccination for re-entry, but it is a good idea to have one anyway. Typhoid inoculation is a good idea, too, especially for anyone wandering in the mountains and drinking water from questionable sources. Immunization records should also include eyeglass prescriptions, in case you need an emergency pair to replace the one you sat on at the top of the *Gross Glockner*.

Money

Exchange rates are in a state of flux, but should stabilize. In Austria, the *schilling* is the common unit, equal to about five cents. Although *groschen* coins are still seen (the smallest is 10 groschen), they are not useful for much. Schilling coins are in 1-, 2-, 5- and 10-schilling denominations, while bills come in 20-, 50-, 100- and 500- schilling sizes.

The German mark is worth about 34 cents. Thus a dollar will buy about three marks. Coins are in 1- and 5-mark denominations, while bills come in 10-, 20- and 50-mark sizes. Penny (*Pfennig*) coins are also used, as are 5-, 10-, and 50-pfennig pieces.

Money can be exchanged anywhere and almost at any time. Railroad stations have counters

marked *Geldwechsel — Cambio — Exchange.*
Changing money is big business in Europe, and
there is usually a line at the counter. Travelers
checks are accepted at all exchange counters, and
at banks. It is usually quicker to exchange money
at one of the railroad-station offices. Banks have a
penchant for paper work, and changing a 20-dollar
bill can be a complicated process. Anywhere, however, you will have to show your passport to the
clerk.

Telephones

Telephoning in Austria is, for the non-German-
speaking person, always a bit of a traumatic experience. However, the dial phone is ubiquitous, so it
is not necessary to try to communicate with an
unsympathetic operator. Local numbers have anywhere from three to six digits. Each area has a five
digit area code which is used only for long distance
calls.

Distances and elevations

The United States is now almost the only country
in the world still tied to the "English" system of
measurement — the inch, foot and mile (not to
mention yard, rod, chain and furlong). In Europe,
all is metric. There is no point in trying to avoid it.
All you can do is to try desperately to start think-
ing in centimeters, meters and kilometers; and in

grams and kilograms. A few ready conversions may be helpful.

There are 2½ centimeters to an inch. The meter is slightly longer than a yard, and there are 1.6 kilometers in a mile. A normal walking pace of three miles per hour is just about five kilometers per hour. One kilometer, a thousand meters, is 3,280 feet.

There are 2.2 pounds in a kilogram; one pound is thus about 0.45 kilogram. There are 28 grams in an ounce. In liquid measure, the liter and quart are very nearly equal, the liter being slightly larger.

Map scales are usually 1:100,000, 1:50,000 or 1:25,000, in which one centimeter equals 1,000, 500 and 250 meters, respectively. For comparison, one of the standard U.S. map scales used on Geological Survey topographic maps is 1:24,000, in which 2½ inches equals a mile.

In much of this book, I have used both measures, metric and English. The only advice I can give is that you should try to think in metric measure; all Europe does.

3. The huts

Nearly five hundred huts are owned and operated in the Austrian Alps by the Austrian and German Alpine Clubs. About two hundred more are operated by the Nature Friends (*Die Naturfreunde*) and the Austrian Tourist Club. Many other private hostels, accessible only by trail, are open to the public. The huts are operated as mountain inns, with accommodations ranging from primitive to elegant (at least for the mountains), and offer the hiker and climber food and shelter at very modest prices. Almost no one camps out in the Alps. At night climbers and hikers can be found enjoying the cameraderie of the huts or getting an early sleep prior to a dawn foray to a nearby peak.

It is impossible to describe the "typical" hut. Size, construction, comfort all vary. The huts have a variety of sleeping accommodations, and all serve hot food. Nearly all of the huts have several small bedrooms with two to six individual beds or bunks. All have dormitory accommodations consisting of gigantic bunks with mattresses placed side-by-side (the *Matratzenlager*) with a pillow and two blankets for each occupant. The capacity of the *Matratzenlager* is flexible: there is always room for one more.

The bunks in the bedrooms have sheets and pillowcases. In the *Matratzenlager*, the hiker either brings his own sheet sleeping sack (one can be made at home from a light cotton blanket) or sleeps rolled up in the blankets. In deference to the fastidious, blankets usually have one end marked *Fuss-ende*, foot end.

Sleeping in the *Matratzenlager* can be quite an experience. First of all, there is always (or so it seems) one person who snores. I am convinced that the hut masters keep one such fellow around just to test the patience of their guests. This is usually not so bad, unless on the night with an overflow crowd you manage to draw the slot right next to the snorer.

Bedroom in Nürnberger Hut

The real experience comes early the next morning. At some secret signal, sometime between four and five o'clock, just as the sky begins to brighten, the *Matratzenlager* fills with loud whispers and the shuffle of feet as early risers pack their rucksacks and prepare to sally forth. Flashes of light streak around the room as last-minute checks are made for misplaced maps or socks. Then the early risers depart for the dining room.

I have never understood why everyone gets up so early. Most of the *Berg-wanderers* are going to the next hut, perhaps a four- or five-hour walk away. They will reach it by noon, and then sit around all afternoon eating, drinking, studying maps and guidebooks. There is something of a mass psychology here, I am sure. Sometimes, if no one gets up early, everyone sleeps until seven. It is all or nothing.

Each hut has one or two common rooms which serve not only as dining rooms, but as places to congregate, study maps, sing and revel after dinner. Typically the tables are large and the benches long, and everyone squeezes together family style at dinnertime. In many of the huts, especially the older ones, a strange-looking tile monster sits in one corner of the common room. It turns out to be a furnace. I have never seen one fired up. But its very presence makes the room seem warmer on a chilly afternoon.

Common room in Nürnberger Hut.

Many of the huts have a *Trockenraum*, a drying-room, downstairs near another furnace or sometimes with special heaters and fans. Here one can hang wet clothing to dry.

Sanitary facilities vary widely. Some huts have running water, hot showers, outlets for electric razors (220 volts AC) and flush toilets. Others have pit toilets and one cold-water tap outside the hut. Most of the huts have at least cold running water inside.

There are certain rules of etiquette that are universally observed in the huts. Some are regulations prescribed by the Alpine Club that operates the hut; others are prescribed by custom. A card describing the regulations, the *Allgemeine Hütten-ordnung des Alpenvereins*, is always posted in a conspicuous place near the door or in the common room. A translation of these regulations can be found in the Appendix.

The first rule, which is always observed, is that hiking boots are not allowed in the sleeping quarters. It is customary to remove boots immediately upon entering, storing them in racks that are usually provided near the door. Boots *may* be allowed in the common room, but slippers or socks are more usual even there. This custom made more sense a few years ago when hob-nailed boots were *de rigeur* for Alpinists. Today, one never sees nailed boots; nevertheless the custom persists, and it does make for cleaner floors. It is a good idea to shed heavy boots anyway, to give tired feet a rest after the trail.

One should arrange for sleeping accommodations as soon as he arrives at the hut. At the height of the season, the beds usually go fast, and assignments are on a first-come, first-served basis. The only exception to this is that at some huts, hikers who are not members of the *Alpenverein* or one of the recognized organizations must wait until six or seven o'clock before being assigned a bed or *Matratzenlager*. Usually one of the waitresses assigns sleeping space, but sometimes the hut master assumes this responsibility. At any rate, *"Haben Sie ein Bett?"* will usually be sufficient.

It is usually a good idea to claim the assigned bed by placing some gear on it to avoid later arguments. And I have found it convenient to arrange the bedding while there is still plenty of light. Some huts do not have electricity, and the *Matratzenlager* can be painfully dark after sunset. Quiet hours are from 10 p.m. until daybreak. There will usually be posted in a conspicuous place the notice *Hüttenruhe ab 2200 Uhr*.

Food and drink

One of the real delights of the Austrian huts is their universally good food and drink. Cooking over an open fire has its joys, but having a hot meal served to you after a hard day's jaunt is a pleasure not to be minimized. Food service is *à la carte*, with the exception of breakfast; and everything, including bread if desired, must be ordered separately.

Breakfast is the universal Continental breakfast, *Frühstück complet*. This consists of three slices of good dark bread, a slab of butter, a portion of jelly or marmalade and a cup or pot of coffee. It is comparatively expensive, usually costing about 20 schillings. In some huts that have a large kitchen it is often possible to change the breakfast routine by ordering bacon and eggs (*Speck mit Spiegeleier*) or even an Austrian pancake (*Pfannkuchen*). Many hikers bring their own breakfast supplies to supplement or supplant the standard *Frühstück*.

Huts vary in the cuisine offered. Some have typed, even printed, menus (*Speisenkarte*). Smaller huts have a choice of only two or three dishes for the evening meal. In these smaller huts, the choices will be announced at about 5 p.m., and one's dinner order must be placed at that time. Late arrivals take pot luck.

Soups are universally good in the huts, and quite inexpensive, usually about six schillings for a bowl of thick pea soup (*Erbsensuppe*) or vegetable soup (*Gemüsesuppe*). There is not much choice: a *Tagessuppe* (soup of the day) and perhaps one other are offered. One of my favorites is *Backerbsensuppe*, a clear soup with specially made croutons the size of peas (hence the name "baked peas") floating in generous quantity.

The main dishes are usually served with a salad and rice or potatoes. Some are prepared to order, but every kitchen prepares several dishes in quantity, such as goulash, hash, or a casserole dish. Following are names and descriptions of the more common dinner dishes:

Wienerschnitzel, the Vienna style breaded veal cutlet, deep fried and served golden brown.

Kalbsbraten, roast veal.

Hackbraten, baked meat loaf.

Champignonomelett, mushroom omelette.

Leberkäs mit Ei. This is a kind of wurst that is fried and usually topped with a fried egg. It is a very tasty dish.

Tirolean Geröstl (also spelled *Gröstl* or *Kröstl*) is a meat and potato hash that is sometimes served with a fried egg.

Gulasch is what we usually call Hungarian goulash. In Austria it is usually very spicy.

Nudelfleisch consists of noodles topped with chopped meat and gravy.

Geräucherter Schinken, fried ham.

Kaiserschmarrn, a kind of pancake, cut in small pieces and glazed with sugar, always served with canned fruit or fruit compote. It is often eaten as a main dish, and is very filling.

In addition to items listed on the menu, all huts are required to serve a dish known as *Bergsteigeressen*, literally "mountain climber food." It is the cheapest item available, presumably so that poor mountain climbers won't starve to death. The dish usually consists of noodles topped with a meat sauce, or a meat hash, heavy on the potatoes, plus a fresh lettuce or cabbage salad. It costs about 20 schillings and is very filling, if not a gourmet's delight. *Alpenverein* regulations specify that it must weigh 500 grams, just over a pound. The huts are permitted to charge a higher price to non-members, but the distinction is rarely made.

It is also possible to purchase a liter or half-liter of hot water to make tea or instant coffee (*"Ein halb-liter tee-wasser, bitte"*). Most of the huts have a great pot of boiling water available throughout the day. Coffee is very expensive in the huts (and elsewhere in Austria) so many hikers bring their own instant, together with sugar and powdered cream. Tea is also expensive when bought by the cup; one tea bag will make a half-liter of tea.

Other items often found on the *Speisekarte* include:

Kompott, fruit compote.

Beilagen, "accompaniments," usually potatoes and salad.

Kartoffeln, potatoes.

Nudeln, noodles.

The huts also provide a variety of beverages for the thirsty hiker. It is probable that more beer is consumed than all other beverages combined, including plain ordinary water. The local bottled brew is always available and is scarcely more expensive than lemonade. The latter is called lim-o-nah-deh and usually seems to be ersatz, made from some kind of concentrate. *Schi-wasser*, another common thirst-quencher, tastes something like Kool-aid, to my palate, anyway. I could never find powdered lemonade mix in Austrian stores, so if you want lemonade as a thirst-quencher on the trail, it is a good idea to bring a supply with you.

Wine is usually available, either red (*Rot-wein*) or white (*Weiss-wein*). It is often a local product and quite acceptable. *Schnapps* is also served, as well as a number of other indigenous hard liquors.

What about the water in the huts and on the trail? I have asked many people in the mountains whether or not they drink water from the streams, and the answers varied. Many seem to be able to walk all day with little or no water; others carry a canteen to hold enough for lunch. However, I am the thirsty type and simply cannot walk all day without liberally quenching my thirst. I have drunk from many high mountain streams with no ill effects. Some caution seems to be in order, though. Animals are plentiful in the mountains, even at high altitudes above timberline. Goats, sheep and cows are everywhere. The higher the elevation, the fewer animals are likely to have been wandering around the streams. Streams with a sizable flow will tend to dilute whatever gets into them. And streams fed directly from glaciers could be expected to be quite potable. However, they also contain considerable glacial silt which should be filtered out before drinking.

Most of the huts have good drinking water from nearby springs or streams known to be safe. The sign *Kein Trinkwasser* above the faucets is a warning that the water is not safe for drinking.

The huts usually have a small commissary from

which it is possible to purchase chocolate bars and cookies for the trail. Many hikers carry a supply of food for lunch as well as breakfast, and supplement meals purchased at the hut with goodies from their own supply. Good Austrian bread can also be purchased at the huts, either by the slice or by the loaf.

An aluminum or plastic box, about eight by twelve inches and four inches deep, is a ubiquitous item in the Alpinist's pack. Squares of cheese, a roll or two of wurst, a package of thin-sliced heavy bread, tea bags and sugar cubes can be packed in this container, to be brought out at breakfast or lunch either on the trail or in the hut. A useful arrangement, one that I recommend.

The hut commissaries also carry picture postcards (*Ansichtskarten*) of the hut and the surrounding peaks. Some also stock postage stamps, but usually not in the proper denomination for airmail to the States. Airmail postage costs four schillings. Postcards so stamped should be marked *Mit Luftpost*. Each hut has its own rubber stamp (*Stempel*), and this is used to imprint the postcards as an identification mark. Many hikers carry little diaries and assiduously collect *Stempel* imprints as proof of their visit.

4. On the trail

People have been hiking and climbing in the Alps for more than a hundred years. Many of the trails in use today were laid out and constructed a half century ago. They have been worn by the tread of countless thousands of hikers' boots. Furthermore, many of these trails are used to move stock up from the valleys in the spring, and back down in the fall. It is not surprising that some of the main trails are more like highways than rough mountain tracks.

The Alpine Clubs have built many of the trails — more than 40,000 km. — signing them and maintaining the walkways. Local residents also keep many trails in repair. In general, they are in very good condition, although occasionally badly eroded stretches can be found where animals or thoughtless and impatient hikers have cut across switchbacks.

It is rare to find a trail junction or terminus that is not adequately signed. The Alpine Clubs install embossed metal plaques that can be read even after the paint has worn off. Distances are universally indicated in terms of time rather than kilometers. (The German word for hour is *Stunde*, abbreviated

Trail signs.

St.) I have found these to be reasonable estimates for an average hiker, i.e., me. At least they give a uniform basis on which to apply one's own weighting factor. It is unlikely that you will be able to cut more than about one-third off the posted times; even a slow walker should be able to accomplish the trails in about one-and-a-half posted times.

The trails are well-marked, usually with paint blazes on rocks. Red is the predominant color, but white is sometimes used and occasionally a combination of red and white stripes may be seen. Some trails are numbered as well. Ducks or cairns (*Steinmann*) are found frequently, especially in rocky stretches where the footway is not so obvious. Sometimes the paint blazes seem so close together that they constitute an eyesore. But one trip in a dense fog will convince you that they are none too close together.

The Alps are steep and rocky. It is not surprising, therefore, that even the main access trails occasionally are routed along narrow ledges bounded by long slippery slopes. Trails sometimes traverse rough boulder fields where a way is marked which hardly qualifies as a foot path.

The Alps are not for the acrophobic. Nevertheless, the main paths are not dangerous for the sure-footed hiker who is well-shod. Some trails are described in the guide books as requiring *Tritt-sicherheit*, literally "step-security." But this designation is primarily intended to keep away the weekend tourist who, with no experience and improper foot-gear, suddenly decides to take a walk in the mountains.

Furthermore, some sections of the trails that are deemed dangerous are secured with steel cables fastened to the rocks with iron pins or pitons. I have found few places where I really thought they were necessary; I usually prefer to steady myself with hand-holds on the rocks. Some of the cables are rather ancient, and I would rather trust my own handhold than a rusted cable attached to pins of dubious security.

The one place in which the American hiker may find himself unprepared by virtue of previous experience is the glacier. Glaciers can be exceedingly dangerous for the inexperienced walker. None of the walks in this book involve glacier crossings that are hazardous. Still, a few words of explanation and caution are in order.

Crevasses, the gaps in glacier ice created by its movement over convex slopes, are often concealed by coverings of snow. Only a suicidal person attempts glacial traverses alone or in an unroped party. Nevertheless, there are portions of glaciers that are not especially dangerous; for example, in the lower reaches where the ice is old, there is no new snow, and any crevasses are easily visible and avoided. Even here, though, it is foolish to attempt to cross old snow bridges that may be left over from winter snowfalls. The bridge could collapse at any time, sending tons of ice and snow — and you — crashing down.

Unless one is planning a glacier crossing, an ice axe (*Pickel*) and crampons (*Steigeisen*) are not necessary; nor is a climbing rope (*Seil*) of any value to the hiking hut-hopper. However, crossing snow-fields and "safe" portions of glaciers can be made easier and more secure with a pair of four-point instep crampons (*Vierzacker*). These are light and easily carried. (Only one of the trips, described in Chapter 9, suggests *Vierzacker*, and even here they are not absolutely necessary. See the description of the Stubai trip.)

If one wants to try his hand (or should I say feet?) at glacier hiking, guides are available at many of the huts. For a modest fee, an Austrian guide will lead you across the glaciers and up the more easily climbed glacial peaks. He will provide the rope, but you must have your own crampons, fitted to your boots, and an ice axe. Arrangements can often be made on the spur of the moment. If you have any notion of attempting such a climb, you should include crampons and ice axe in your kit.

Since we are discussing Alpine dangers, this is perhaps a good place to indicate the universal Alpine distress signal. It is six signals spaced evenly in one minute, then a minute pause, and the six signals are repeated. The reply to the distress signal is a series of three signals spaced evenly in one minute, repeated after a minute's pause. The signals may be visual or audible. It is a good idea to carry a whistle and a flashlight for emergency use.

If you are injured and need assistance in the mountains, you will find that the rescue effort is efficient and experienced. You will, however, probably be charged for the service, unless you are a member of the *Alpenverein*. Membership includes insurance to pay for rescue efforts and recuperation expenses. (More about Club membership later.)

As indicated in Chapter 3, most Alpine hikers have a thing about starting at the crack of dawn. This may be necessary if the day's journey is long, or if it is necessary or desirable to cross a certain stretch of trail before the sun hits it. But I have never really understood the rationale for such early rising. So set your own timetable and pace. Don't be stampeded into something just because everyone else is doing it. By the same token, elevations in the Austrian Alps are generally lower than in the High Sierra of California. Thus, acclimatization to the thin air is somewhat quicker.

Maps and Guidebooks

There is an embarrassing abundance of trail maps

and guidebooks for most sections of the Austrian Alps. And they all seem to be good, superior to many of the maps and guides available for American mountains. The maps prepared by the Austrian government are excellent and accurate. They have been made using aerial photogrammetric techniques and are available for the entire country on a scale of 1:50,000. Some measure of the importance of Alpine hiking is indicated by the fact that government maps are published in a special series, *Wanderkarte*, with trails, huts and other information of value to the hiker and climber included. The only drawback is that the map boundaries are determined by the standard grid system and therefore one may find that even a short hike requires three or four adjoining maps for complete coverage. They are published by the *Bundesamt für Eich- und Vermessungswesen (Landesaufnahme)* in Vienna, and are available in many bookstores and even at some of the huts. The cost: 25 schillings per quadrangle. Each map contains an index to the entire series, so locating a particular quadrangle is an easy matter.

The Austrian and German Alpine Clubs also publish a series of topographic maps designed for the hiker and mountain climber. Although they are based on the government survey maps, they have been redrafted and cover natural mountain groups, rather than the arbitrary quadrangles of the official surveys. Most have been published at a scale of 1:25,000. They usually contain more up-to-date trail information than the government maps. They are available from either the Austrian *Alpenverein* in Innsbruck or the German *Alpenverein* in Munich, as well as in bookstores specializing in maps and books for hikers.

Several commercial cartographers also publish trail maps. Freytag-Berndt in Vienna publishes a series at a scale of 1:100,000. Heinz Fleischman in Innsbruck publishes the *Kompass Wanderkarte* series at scale 1:50,000. Both of these series are widely available throughout the hiking regions in Austria. They are folded to pocket size, are printed in full color and have good legends in English as well as German and French. For the trail hiker, the *Kompass Wanderkarten* are perhaps the best choice. They do not have as much detail as the other maps (100-meter contour intervals, for example) but because of this are somewhat easier to read. All of the maps are good, however, and the choice is to a large extent one of personal preference.

One special map deserves attention. It is the *Schutzhüttenkarte* of the *Alpenverein*. This covers the entire Alpine region of Austria at a scale of 1:600,000 (approximately ten miles to the inch) and shows the locations of all of the huts of the *Alpenverein* as well as many run by clubs and privately-operated huts open to the public. The map is also a good general guide to the mountain regions of the Alps, and it delineates the boundaries of the various mountain ranges and groups. A useful companion to this and, indeed, keyed to it, is the *Taschenbuch der Alpenvereins-Mitglieder* (Alpine Club members' handbook). It carries a complete description of all of the *Alpenverein* huts, and many others as well. Included is information on location, height, accommodations, operating season, and so forth. It costs less than a dollar and is a most useful handbook.

Many of the maps have legends printed in German, French, and English. But some do not, and to aid in interpreting map symbols, a list of the most common terms is included in the glossary. Graded and marked trails are generally shown in red. A solid line usually indicates a well-marked graded path; sometimes these are narrow roads. (On some maps, a solid red line is used to indicate ski trails.) A broken line indicates a marked, graded mountain trail. A dotted line indicates a marked way, usually not graded. Rougher, sometimes poorly marked paths may be marked by a dotted black line.

Although maps and guidebooks are generally accurate and up-to-date, it never hurts to inquire of fellow hikers or hut masters about specific trail conditions. It has been my experience, however, that any trail indicated on a map in red is well-

marked and easy to follow. An exception, of
course, might occur in early summer before all of
the snow has melted, or during foggy conditions,
which are not uncommon in the Alps.

Although most guidebooks are in German, even
a modest reading knowledge of the language is sufficient to enable one to glean most of the necessary
trail information from them. They provide detailed
descriptions of the trails and paths as well as the
routes up the various peaks.

The largest publisher of trail guides is Rudolf
Rother in Munich. This company specializes in
Alpine books and every bookstore in the Alpine
region carries a shelf of them. Many regions have
local guidebooks, written and published locally.
These may usually be obtained in bookstores and
tourist shops in the towns nearby. Most include
trail maps, but these are no substitute for the maps
described earlier. In the chapters containing detailed tour descriptions, I have listed the maps and
guidebooks available for each region.

One guidebook should receive special mention.
The Austrian National Tourist Office publishes a
48-page pamphlet: *Mountain Rambles in Austria*.
Available in English, it contains useful information
on guides, climbing schools, cable cars, and so
forth, in addition to brief descriptions of suggested
hiking and climbing trips of various lengths. It may
be obtained free from the New York branch of

the Austrian National Tourist Office, 545 Fifth
Avenue, New York, New York 10017.

Membership in the Alpine Clubs

Anyone who hikes in the Alps and uses the facilities of the Alpine huts should be a member of
either the Austrian or German Alpine Club. Membership is open to all upon payment of the entrance fee and dues for a year. Membership confers
a number of advantages on the Alpine hiker. Hut
fees are less for the member, sufficiently so that a
week or two in the huts will save enough money to
pay for the membership fee. Also, as may be seen
in the General Hut Regulations in Appendix I,
members have priorities on accommodations and
other perquisites. Furthermore, members are
covered by liability insurance, and, in case of an
accident in the mountains, the insurance pays costs
of search and rescue (which are not free in
Europe), and costs of recuperation.

Even more important, perhaps, is the need to
support the organizations that do so much to make
hiking and climbing in the Alps possible. The two
clubs together maintain more than 40,000 kilometers of trails in the Austrian and Bavarian Alps.
They publish trail maps, organize mountain climbing schools, arrange tours, publish yearbooks and
act as clearinghouses for all kinds of mountaineering information. This may sound like a lot of ac-

tivity for such specialized clubs, but not when you realize that the combined membership is nearly 500,000.

Joining one of the clubs is a simple matter of filling out an application at the main headquarters in Innsbruck or Munich, submitting two passport-size photos and paying the fees: 120 schillings annual dues, plus 25 schillings entrance fee, a total of about six dollars. The Innsbruck office is at 15 Wilhelm-Greil Strasse, about three blocks from the railroad station. In Munich, the German Alpine Club headquarters is at 5 Praterinsel. The two organizations are closely affiliated and it matters little which one you join.

5. What to take, what to wear

No self-respecting European alpinist would dare be seen on the trail in anything but the ubiquitous knickers and knee-length socks. Knickers may be the appropriate clothing for the rock-climber, but they are not necessary for the hiker. Wear what you find comfortable hiking in the Sierras, Cascades, Rockies or White Mountains. The only criteria are that clothes be comfortable and sturdy.

Although Alpine hikers have not given up knickers, they have given up hob-nailed boots. One *never* sees nailed boots, the much-superior Vibram lug sole having replaced them completely. Be sure that your boots are sturdy enough to withstand the punishment of an Alpine hike. Nothing can spoil a hike faster than uncomfortable, poorly-made footgear.

Austria is famous for its good footwear; and every shoe store carries a variety of mountain boots. Wearing new boots on a mountain hike is risky, but if you are careful to purchase a pair that fits well, there should be no trouble. Repairs to hiking shoes are easier to obtain in Austria than in the U.S. I had the misfortune to have a sole start to separate from the counter while on the way down to Innsbruck from the Stubai. But I was able to find a *Schuhreparaturen* that could make an overnight emergency repair. (This was in the shoe store, Stiefel-Kater, on Meraner Strasse in Innsbruck.)

Since boots are verboten in the huts, some kind of light-weight slipper or shoe is necessary. Of course, one can wander around in socks, but this is hard on them. Slipper sox are good, but any kind of light-weight slipper that will fit over the heavy socks you are wearing will do. There is something to be said for taking a pair of tennis shoes instead of slippers. Although they are somewhat heavier, they can be used on the trail in an emergency, if one's shoes fall apart (as has happened to me on one occasion, twenty miles back in the Sierra, *without* extra shoes).

Rain is frequent in the Alps, so good rain-wear is essential. My favorite piece of rain gear is a cagoule made of water-proofed nylon. It is knee-length, has a draw-string around the bottom and is large enough so that when seated, the knees can be drawn up inside it. With the drawstring tied, it makes a fine emergency bivouac shelter. It also has a hood, and in mine, the cloth is doubled around the shoulders for extra protection. It is windproof and excellent for wear on cold days. For safety, it is a good idea to choose a bright color that can be readily seen from a distance.

The anorak, a light but sturdy hooded parka, is

the most common outer garment seen in the Alps. It is relatively short and affords little protection to the legs in a rainstorm, but does act as a windbreaker. Wind protection is important, and any parka or outer garment should be windproof. Ski parkas are not uncommon, but often they are not waterproof, and have the disadvantage of being all or nothing. It is better to have a lightweight outer garment and a warm sweater or down vest that can be worn separately or together, as needed. My choice would be a down shirt or vest plus a cagoule. Together these weigh about two pounds and will provide good protection from sudden storms. It should be remembered that most hiking is done above timberline. Even in summer, snowstorms may occur above about two thousand meters.

There is much to be said for some extra protection for the lower half of one's body. Light-weight nylon or plastic rainchaps keep the legs dry. A pair of light-weight woolen long-johns weighs about a half-pound and can come in very handy for hut wear if one's trousers are soaked from a cold rain.

Warm mittens are better than gloves, although almost anything will do. An extra pair of socks, and an extra set of underwear completes the clothing list.

The absolutely universal backpack in the Alps is the low-slung rucksack. It is an abomination for trail walking; with any weight in it at all, it pulls the shoulders back. For rock climbers it has the advantage of keeping the weight low, and not interfering with a backward tilt of the head, as a frame pack may do if packed high. I found few hikers in the Alps who would defend the rucksack; many complained bitterly about it. The only thing that makes it acceptable at all is that the load is usually light, and so the disadvantages of bad weight distribution are not so important. But in central Europe, it is the only thing available in the sporting goods stores.

The American frame pack is the best choice for trail hiking in the Alps or anywhere. It is ubiquitous in the streets of Europe, a standard cargo carrier of the American student-tourist. But it is not seen often in the mountains. My own frame pack was often the object of interest and some admiration. One suggestion: it is better to have a pack without the highest cross-bar, at least if it interferes with tilting your head back. This is not important if you intend to stick to the trails. But if you plan to do any rock scrambling at all, it is better to have complete freedom of movement of the head.

The pack need not be large, for not so much gear must be carried as on a back-country trip requiring cooking gear and sleeping bags. Without such gear, what is left to put in the pack? Plenty, it seems. Besides extra clothing, I have found the following items useful. Some of them are absolutely essential.

Maps and trail guide can be kept in a plastic bag or in a map case with a plastic window. A small *compass* will come in handy to help you orient maps. It could be essential if you become lost.

Each party of hikers should have a *first aid kit*. Most of the commercially available kits are useless, and have all the wrong things in them. A better idea is to get a small aluminum box and assemble your own kit. I carry a kit that has about 45 different items. Even with a first-aid manual (*Mountaineering Medicine*, by Fred Darvill, published by the Skagit Mountain Rescue Unit, Inc.), these items pack into a 4" x 6½" x 3" aluminum box. The weight is one and a half pounds. It is not necessary to carry such an extensive and complete kit, but certain items should be in every kit. These include bandaids of various sizes, moleskin, Ace bandage, tweezers, small scissors, adhesive tape, aspirin, small cake of soap, Lomotil (a prescription diarrhea preventive), sunburn cream, first-aid cream, any special drugs or prescriptions that your physician recommends.

Personal effects can also be packed into a small aluminum container or carried in a cloth bag. *Soap* is an absolute necessity. A *washcloth* can serve double duty as a towel as well. Alternatively, a diaper makes a good light-weight towel. *Lip pomade* should be carried. A toothbrush (do you really need toothpaste?) and a comb are light and take little room. A small amount of toilet paper is useful, not only for emergencies but also to clean spectacles, knife blades, and so forth. A razor or other personal necessities can well go in this kit.

A small *flashlight* is an absolute necessity, not only for the emergency of being caught out after dark, but for seeing one's way around the hut at night after the lights have been turned off.

Although most of your meals will be eaten in one of the huts, some food must be taken for trail lunches and emergencies. As described in the chapter on the huts, most hikers carry a plastic or aluminum box in which to carry lunch items. Many include a knife and small cutting board, but the latter is not really necessary. The pack should include some sort of canteen and cup. I find that a light plastic one-quart bottle with a cup-top serves admirably, and is lighter than an aluminum canteen. If you are traveling in a group of three or four, you might consider taking a small kerosene, gasoline or alcohol stove to heat soup or tea water for lunch. The only difficulty is in purchasing fuel; sometimes it is difficult to find. Alcohol (*Spiritus*) can usually be obtained in a drug store (*Drogerie*) or a hardware store (*Eisenwaren*).

You will need some place safe and dry to keep

your passport, inoculation record, and travelers checks. A small plastic bag will serve admirably.

For rainy and foggy days on which you are confined to the hut, some equipment for self-entertainment is desirable. A deck of cards or a paperback book will really be appreciated. There is usually a supply of reading material in the huts but it is all in German — a file of climbing journals and publications of the Alpine clubs.

Your camera film can also be kept in a plastic bag. Color film is readily available (*Farb-film für Dias*).

That is about all that is necessary. Whatever else you take is up to you. Although the pack is light by American back-packing standards, there is little point in adding on useless extras just to "bring it up to weight!" Enjoy your light pack.

6. The German language

German is the language of the Austrian Alps. This is true of the main eastern portion of the Swiss Alps, and of course, the Bavarian Alps in southern Germany. Most people who have regular contact with the traveling public speak at least some English, and many are quite fluent. In the mountains, this may not be true. Many of the huts are run by local residents who have little contact with English-speaking hikers. But even here, it is surprising how little verbal communication is absolutely necessary.

So, even though you may get by with little or no knowledge of German, it will be a distinct help to have some elementary grasp of the spoken colloquial language. A pocket phrase book, such as the Berlitz *Phrase Book for Travelers*, is a great help. The glossary at the end of this book contains words that are likely to be found on trail maps, in the huts, and on trail signs. (Translations of food items are in Chapter 3.)

Though German grammar is difficult, German pronunciation is quite easy. Words are pronounced as they are spelled, and once a few basic rules are learned, any word can be spoken understandably.

The worst hurdle, perhaps, is the German penchant for combining related words into a long connected string, such as *Gepäcksaufbewahrung* (literally, baggage watching-over) or *Hauptbahnhof* (main railroad station). The trick is to take the word one piece at a time, pronouncing it as if it were really several words. The difficulty, of course, is in recognizing the component parts, and that comes only with some knowledge of the language.

Most of the letters are pronounced about as they are in English. The few exceptions give the language its distinctive sound. These should be learned and practiced. The main pronunciation rules follow:

ch like sh, but more off the back of the tongue

z ts; *Zug* (train) is pronounced Tsook

s at the beginning of a word as z: *Sie* is pronounced zee; otherwise as in English

v is soft, as the English f

w is like the English v; *Volkswagen* = Folksvagen

ä broad, as in say; *Käse* = kayzeh

ö pronounced as er; *schön* = shern

ü as ew in few; *für* = few'r

eu as oy; *Feuer* = foyer

j is always soft, like y; *Joch* = yoch

ee is the broad a; *See* is Zay

Many plurals are formed by adding *n*: *eine*

Karte, zwei Karten; eine Hütte, zwei Hütten. Others
are formed by umlauting the vowel and adding *e*:
ein Kamm, zwei Kämme; ein Raum, zwei Räume.
A few have the same plural as singular: *Führer,
Führer.*

II. Trips

MAP SYMBOLS

╫╪═╫─┼┼┼┼┼┼	RAILROAD WITH STATION
══════════	ROAD
━ ━ ━ ━ ━	TRAIL
∼∼∼∼∼∼	STREAM
⸜⸜⸜⸜⸜⸜	SLOPE OR MOUNTAIN
▲ 2863 PEAK	ELEVATION IN METERS
■┼┼┼┼┼┼┼┼┼┼┼■	CABLEWAY-GOODS ONLY
■•••••••••■	GONDOLA CABLEWAY
⌂	ALPINE HUT OR INN
☁	LAKE
■	HUT OR BARN
)(	PASS

7. The Schladminger Tauern: lakes, forests and mountains

East of Innsbruck, toward Salzburg and Vienna, the Alps are somewhat lower and less rugged than they are in western Austria. The easternmost glaciers are to be found in the Hohe Tauern, on the slopes of the Gross Venediger (3674 m.), and the Gross Glockner (3737 m.) and their neighbors. But if the peaks here are a little less high and forbidding than the Stubai Alps, described in Chapter 9, they are that much more accessible to the ordinary hiker. The Niedere Tauern (of which the Schladminger Tauern is one part) are such mountains.

The Niedere Tauern lie south of the Enns River and stretch for 150 kilometers, from Bischofshofen and Badgastein in the west nearly to Graz in the east. Near the center of this region, and just south of Schladming, lie the Schladminger Tauern. They are friendly mountains, clothed with forest on their lower slopes; the valleys are dotted with farms and tiny villages. The upper slopes are bald and grassy, and while steep, are not so imposing as those farther west. And the region is dotted with small lakes which heighten the scenic interest. In the heart of the region lies the spectacular Klaffer-kessel, a heavily eroded high basin with rocky crags interspersed with dozens of tiny tarns and small lakes. With its relatively low elevations (the highest pass on this hike is about 2000 meters), the walking is not too demanding and the acclimatization to altitude easy.

Geologically, the Niedere Tauern belong to the central Alpine fold or sheet just south of the band of limestone mountains that stretches from the Lechtaler Alps in the west to Vienna in the east. The Dachstein group, just north of Schladming, are part of this bright range of chalk mountains, and indeed provide spectacular views along much of the route. The rocks in the Schladminger Tauern are crystalline and rich in minerals. In fact, mining started in this region in the 13th century and continued actively until the beginning of the present century. Some of the old workings can still be seen from points on the route.

Timberline lies at 1800 meters, about 100 meters higher than in the Dachstein mountains to the north. Larch and spruce are the timberline trees, although mountain pine (*Pinus cembra*) climbs higher, growing in a nearly prostrate form. On lower slopes, such hardwoods as the red beech, alder and other broad-leaved species are common. Game is plentiful. The region is known for its antelope (*Gemse*). Red deer are not uncommon, and the smaller marmot abounds.

Schladming is the hub of the region, an attractive town with a population of 3,500. It lies on the rail line from Bischofshofen to Graz, and is easily accessible from either Innsbruck or Salzburg. For the rail trip direct from Munich, it is better to go via Wörgl on the main route to Innsbruck than to go via Salzburg. Although the actual distance is slightly less via Salzburg, the connections are not as good. There is through service from Wörgl to Schladming; the trip takes about three hours. Wörgl is about an hour and a half from Munich, and less than an hour from Innsbruck by the express trains.

For the trip detailed in this chapter, the hiker should disembark at Haus, the second stop east of Schladming. From there, a taxi may be taken to Bodensee in the Seewigtal, the point of departure for Hans Wödl Hut. (The stationmaster at Haus will telephone for a taxi if you ask him. The fare to Bodensee is about 100 schillings.)

Accommodations are plentiful in Schladming; it is both a summer and winter resort town. Information may be obtained from the *Fremdenverkehrsverein*, the tourist office on Pfarrgasse, one block from the town square. A town map may also be obtained from this office, showing the location of tourist accommodations as well as major commercial facilities. There is a 110-bed youth hostel just off the east end of the square, on Coburgstrasse. The railroad station is about a half-mile northwest

The main square in Schladming.

of the town square, on Langegasse between the railroad and the river. Incidentally, the local buses use the town square rather than the railroad station as terminus.

A number of maps and guidebooks are available. The best trail map is probably Kompass Wanderkarte No. 31, *Radstadt-Schladming*, at a scale of 1:50,000. Freytag-Berndt Wanderkarte No. 20 also covers the entire route, but at a scale of 1:100,000. The new Alpenvereinkarte, *Niedere Tauern* II, No. 61, at a scale of 1:50,000 has the most detail of any, but cuts off a portion of the beginning of the route. (There is an old AV map, dated 1924, that should be avoided.) Austrian Federal survey Map 127, *Schladming*, also covers the area.

Rudolf Rother publishes the Alpenvereinsführer, *Schladminger und Radstädter Tauern*. There is also a locally published guidebook: *Schladming-Dachstein und Tauerngebiet*, available from the Ernst Kortschak bookstore in Schladming. (The store is on the Postgasse, just around the corner from the main square, in the center of town.) Both of these are, of course, in German. So far as I know, there is no English language guidebook available. However, a short but interesting article on the "Huts of the Schladminger Tauern" by Martin G. and Barbara B. Larrabee was published in the June 1971 issue of *Appalachia*.

From Haus to Hans Wödl Hut

The road to Bodensee, the start of the trail, leads south from the village of Aich, about 2 kilometers east of the Haus railroad station, which in turn is about 10 kilometers east of Schladming. There is a bus that runs from Schladming, but if you are traveling by train, the most convenient stop is at Haus, from which a taxi may be taken to Bodensee. The trail starts at the parking lot at the end of the Seewigtal road and leads in a few yards to the north end of the lake and a small inn, Wirtshaus Fink. There are fine views of the cascades and

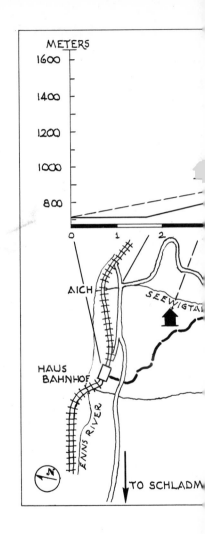

Haus or Aich to
Hans Wödl Hut

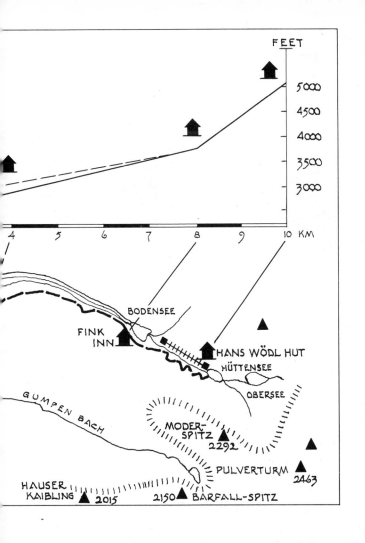

Hans Wödl Hut.

waterfall above Bodensee from this point.

Crossing the outlet to the west side of the lake, the trail continues around the west shore to the south end where the bottom station of the cableway to the hut is located. (Packs can be carried to the hut on the cableway for a fee, but service is irregular.) From this point, the trail ascends sharply through weeds on a series of switchbacks, staying on the right (west) side of the valley. Finally it levels off somewhat and reaches the Hans Wödl Hut at the north end of Hüttensee.

The hut is in a most scenic location, on a small knoll at the end of the lake. It is a rustic building, set in the trees (well below timberline) and is rather reminiscent of the older huts of the Appalachian Mountain Club in the White Mountains of New Hampshire. Although it is owned and operated by the Preintaler Alpine Society of Vienna, it is open to the public, and Alpenverein members are charged members' rates.

Walking time from Bodensee to Hans Wödl Hut: 1 hour. Walking time from Haus or Aich to Bodensee, 2 hours. (There is a direct path from Haus railroad station to Bodensee that avoids the road in the valley, but I cannot vouch for it. You should make local inquiry. It is marked on the Kompass map and should not be hard to find.)

Hans Wödl Hut: 1528 meters. Built 1897. 18 beds, 40 *Matratzenlager*.

From Hans Wödl Hut to Preintaler Hut

The Robert Höfer Steig, a well-marked graded path, leads from Hans Wödl Hut to Preintaler Hut over Neualmscharte. It was built in 1907 and 1908 by the Preintaler Alpein Gesellschaft to connect the two huts that had been built ten years earlier. It leads past several scenic high mountain lakes and affords excellent views of the Dachstein to the north and the Hochwildstelle and Waldhorn to the south.

The trail leads south from the hut along the west bank of Huttensee. At the upper end, it ascends steeply to the outlet of Obersee, the highest of the

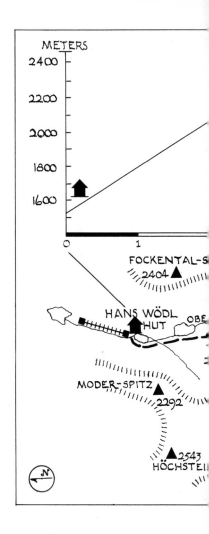

METERS

2400

2200

2000

1800

1600

0   1

FOCKENTAL-S
2404 ▲

HANS WÖDL
HUT   OBE

MODER-SPITZ ▲
2292

▲2543
HÖCHSTEI

Hans Wödl Hut to
Preintaler Hut

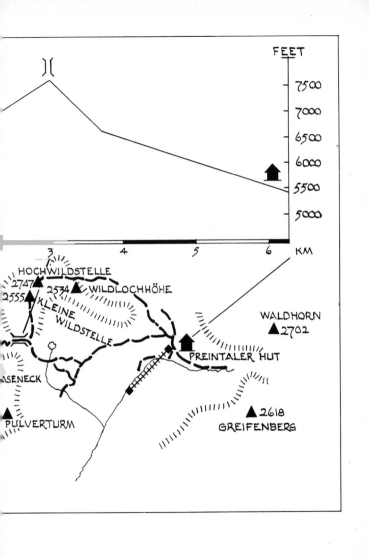

Waterfall near Hans Wödl Hut.

three lakes in Seewigtal. From here it ascends over open slopes, zig-zagging its way up a talus slope to Neualmscharte, the low point on the ridge connecting Hochstein with Hochwildstelle. (A red-marked path leads left up the ridge to the summit of the Kleine Wildstelle, 2577 m, 10 min.; the route leads further in a half-hour to the summit of Wildlochscharte and thence down to Preintaler Hut. A guidebook should be consulted for that route description.)

From Neualmscharte, the trail descends sharply, crossing a tributary of the Riesach Brook. After climbing the south bank, a trail junction is reached. The right branch descends to Riesach Bach at Kerschbaumer Alm. The main path continues south and in a few hundred yards, another junction is reached, the right-hand trail leading north-west to Schladminger Hut. In about a half hour, another trail comes in from the left, the route from Wildlochscharte and Hochwildstelle. In about ten minutes, the Riesach Bach is crossed and the trail turns sharply right just before the Preintaler Hut.

Time from Hans Wödl Hut to Obersee: ¾ h.; to Neualmscharte, 2½ h; to Preintaler Hut, 4 h. Marked red and red/white.

Preintaler Hut. 1656 meters. Built 1891. Open 15 June to 30 September. 16 beds, 40 *Matratzenlager*.

From Preintaler Hut to Golling Hut

The route from Preintaler to Golling Hut passes through the wild and spectacular Klafferkessel, a high granite basin containing dozens of tiny lakes and ponds. The basin is heavily eroded, and there are many sharp towers, ridges, blocks and other erosional features scattered throughout the basin. It is one of the scenic highlights of any trip in the Schladminger Tauern.

The trail from Preintaler Hut leads southwest, sharply ascending the steep slopes of the Lämmerkar, crosses the Waldhorn brook and soon reaches a trail junction. The left branch continues southward up the Lämmerkar to the Kapuzinersee. Take the right branch, which climbs steeply over talus to the Unter Klafferscharte (2286 m.), the gateway to the Klafferkessel.

From here, the trail winds around through the basin, passing between granite blocks and along the shores of many of the ponds, the largest of which is the Ober Klaffersee, about 300 meters long. Shortly thereafter, the trail begins the ascent to the Upper Klafferscharte (2516 m.), a narrow pass on the Greifenberg ridge. At the pass, the trail turns sharply right and ascends the left (south) side of the ridge, reaching the summit about 15 minutes from the pass. The summit (2618 m.) affords fine views of the Schladminger Tauern.

Rock formations in the Klafferkessel.

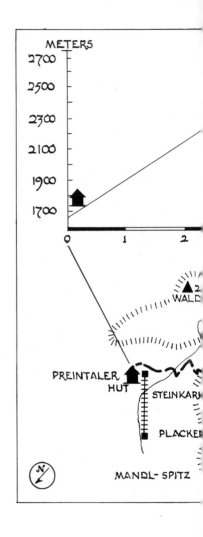

Preintaler Hut to
Golling Hut

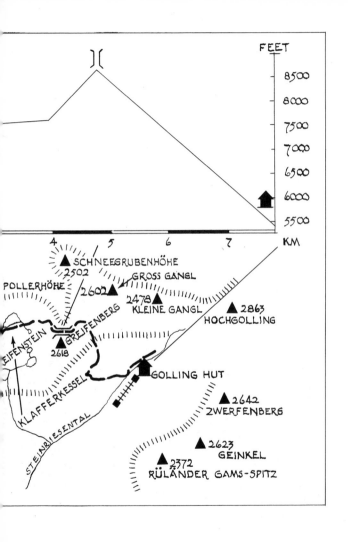

Dropping sharply down south ridge, the broad Greifenberg Sattel with its small lake is soon reached. The trail swings westward and descends sharply toward the Steinriesen Valley. After passing several small but spectacular waterfalls, the trail turns left (southwestward) and continues down the slope to Golling Hut.

Time from Preintaler Hut to Unter Klafferscharte: 2 h; to Greifenberg, 3 h; to Golling Hut, 5 h. Marked red throughout.

Golling Hut. 1650 meters. Built 1904 by the Alpine Gesellschaft Preintaler. Open 15 June to 30 September. 12 beds, 31 *Matratzenlager.*

Preintaler Hut.

Gollingwinkel.

From Golling Hut to Landwiersee Hut

The route over Gollingscharte, close under the massive dome of Hochgolling, is one of impressive views and great scenic beauty. The great natural amphitheatre, the Gollingwinkel, close under the massive north face of Hochgolling, is surely one of the finest of its kind in the Austrian Alps: a flat grassy meadow surrounded by towering rock walls on three sides, a U-shaped glacial basin that could make a Texas-sized coliseum. And Hochgolling itself, the tallest mountain in the Schladminger Tauern, can be climbed easily from Gollingscharte, over which our route passes.

Landwiersee Hut and Lake.

From the hut, the well-trod path leads south up the Steinriesen brook, quickly reaching the Upper Steinwender Alm in the Gollingwinkel. After crossing a flat meadow, past several fallen-down stone huts, the trail turns westward and ascends a broad gully to Gollingscharte (2326 m.). From this point, Landwiersee Hut can be seen just south of west, although the lake itself is obscured by an intervening ridge. From the pass, Hochgolling may be climbed via a well-marked and not-difficult route. The route climbs alternately up the ridge and the west (right) side of the ridge to a junction. The right-hand trail, the so-called "normal" route, continues along the west side of the ridge, finally turning eastward, attaining the ridge's crest a few yards below the summit. Time from Gollingscharte, 1 h.

From Gollingscharte, the trail to Landwiersee Hut descends over loose talus for a short distance to a trail junction. The left branch leads down to the upper end of the Goriachtal and joins a cart track that climbs back up to the hut. The easier way is to the right, along the "high route." This route requires sure footing as it traverses the steep south slopes of the Sam Spitz-Zwerfenberg ridge. Contouring the slope for about a half-mile, the hiker reaches a trail junction. The left-hand fork angles down toward Landwiersee Hut. The right fork remains on the contour and proceeds to Trockenbrot (dry-bread!) Scharte and Keinprecht

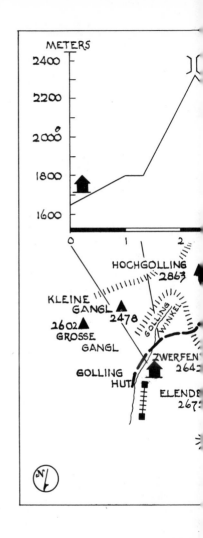

Golling Hut to
Landwiersee Hut
and Keinprecht Hut

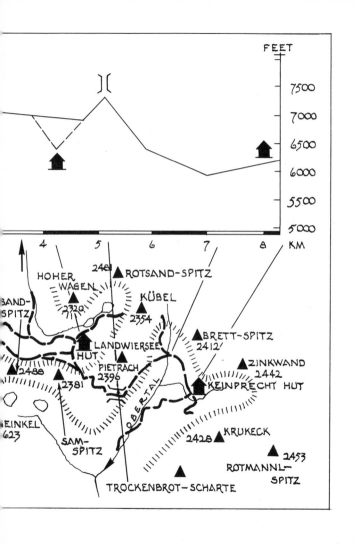

Hut. From this junction, Landwiersee Hut may be reached in about fifteen minutes.

The hut is the smallest and most primitive in the region. It is a long, low stone bulding, with the common room at the south end, a barn at the north end, and the hut master's quarters in between. Sleeping quarters are on the second floor. The hut also has a novel feature that I have seen nowhere else: a pit toilet on the second floor. The hut is in a beautiful location, with the two small glacial lakes, the Unter and Ober Landwiersee, nearby.

Time from Golling Hut to Gollingscharte, 2 h; to Landwiersee Hut, 3½ h.

Landwiersee Hut: 2030 meters. Open early July to mid-September. 6 beds, 19 *Matratzenlager.* Primitive facilities.

From Landwiersee Hut to Keinprecht Hut

The route between these two huts affords spectacular views, especially of the Dachstein Mountains to the north. The distance is short. If time is pressing, and especially if Hochgolling is climbed, it is possible to avoid Landwiersee Hut by taking the right fork on the high route described in the previous section. Alternatively, a brief stop may be made at the Landwiersee Hut for an afternoon snack, at an additional cost in trail time of less than half an hour.

From the hut, the red-marked trail leads north-ward, retracing the path for a few yards to a trail junction, then swings northwestward and ascends over glacial moraine toward the Trockenbrot-scharte. Just before the steep portion of the climb, the "high route" enters from the right (sign). The left branch of the trail ascends the steep east slope of the pass, soon reaching it after several switch-backs. The view from the top is spectacular. To the north, the panorama of the Hochstein Mountains looms into view. To the southeast, the entire mass of Hochgolling dominates the view, with its three smaller neighbors, the nearly identical cones of the Steinkarleck (2637 m.), Weisshohe (2646 m.) and Kasereck (2740 m.) marching to the south.

From the pass, the trail descends sharply on a series of switchbacks, then turns sharply left along the slope of Pietrach (2396 m.). The trail continues to slope downward, swinging in a wide arc to the southwest, finally reaching the low point where it crosses the Obertal Brook. From here, the trail turns northwestward, climbing gently past an aban-doned hut, then climbing more steeply a few hun-dred yards to Keinprecht Hut.

High above the hut, on the slopes of the Zink-wand, are the abandoned tunnels and remains of centuries-old mines. They can be reached by a part-ly obscure trail that leads to the Holzschartl from the hut. Inquiry concerning the location of the

Hochgolling from Landwiersee.

mines should be made at the hut.

Time from Landwiersee Hut to Trockenbrot-scharte, ½ h; to Obertal Brook crossing, 2 h; to Keinprecht Hut, 2¼ h.

Keinprecht Hut: 1872 meters. Open 15 June to 25 September. 4 beds, 30 *Matratzenlager*.

From Keinprecht Hut to Ignaz-Mattis Hut

From Keinprecht Hut, the walker has the choice of heading valleyward to the bus-stop at Hopfriesen, or spending another day by crossing over the Sauberg-Krukeck ridge to Giglachsee and Ignaz-Mattis Hut. Unter Giglachsee is the largest lake in

Keinprecht Hut.

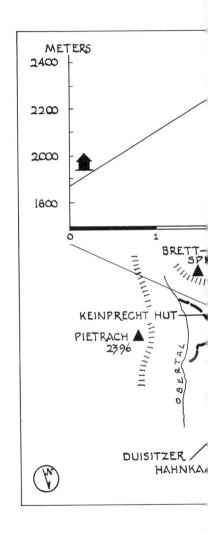

METERS
2400
2200
2000
1800

0   1

BRETT-
SP

KEINPRECHT HUT

PIETRACH ▲
2396

OBERTAL

DUISITZER
HAHNKA

Keinprecht Hut to
Ignaz-Mattis Hut

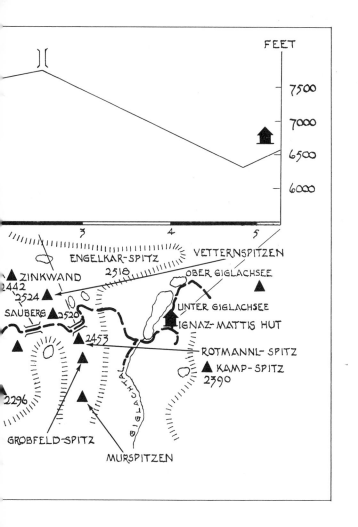

FEET

7500

7000

6500

6000

3   4   5

ENGELKAR-SPITZ   VETTERNSPITZEN

2518   OBER GIGLACHSEE

ZINKWAND
2442
2524

SAUBERG   2520   UNTER GIGLACHSEE

IGNAZ-MATTIS HUT

2453   ROTMANNL-SPITZ

KAMP-SPITZ
2390

2296

GROBFELD-SPITZ

MURSPITZEN

GIGLACHTL.

the region, and will repay one's effort to reach it, if time permits.

The trail leads north from the hut and switch-backs up the south slopes of Krukeck, then turns left (west) across a glacial cirque south of the summit. The trail ascends the slope to Krukeckscharte (2303 m.), crossing over into the north-facing Buckelkar. Then it climbs gently over a rocky slope of Sauberg (2520 m.), which rises to the south of the trail, and reaches Rotmandlscharte (2433 m.). Spectacular views of the Dachstein Mountains to the north are to be had from the pass. Hochgolling looms to the east, while several small glacial lakes nestle in their cirques deep below the pass to the northeast. From this spot, each direction presents magnificent views. Take a few minutes to enjoy them. The trail proceeds over the low summit of Rotmandlspitz (2453 m.) and switchbacks its way down to Vetternkar, with its two small glacial lakes. Crossing the bottom of the cirque, the trail reaches the outlet of Unter Giglachsee, which it crosses, then proceeds a short distance to the hut.

Time from Keinprecht Hut to Krukeckscharte, 1½ h; to Rotmandlscharte, 2 h; to Ignaz-Mattis Hut, 3 h.

Ignaz-Mattis Hut: 1986 meters. Built 1910. Open 15 June to 25 September. 14 beds, 40 *Matratzenlager*.

If the decision is to descend to Hopfriesen directly

from Keinprecht Hut, retrace the trail to Obertal Brook for about a hundred yards to a trail junction. Follow the left branch down a small gully, to the main brook, keeping to its left side. After a short distance, the trail crosses to the right side and continues to the roadhead at Eschach Alm. The road is followed for 2 kilometers to the bus stop at Hopfriesen.

Walking time about 1½ h.

From Ignaz-Mattis Hut to Hopfriesen and Schladming

The trail from the hut to Hopfriesen stays close to

Giglachsee and vicinity of Ignaz-Mattis Hut.

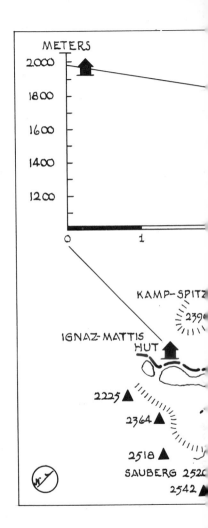

Ignaz-Mattis Hut to
Hopfriesen and
Schladming

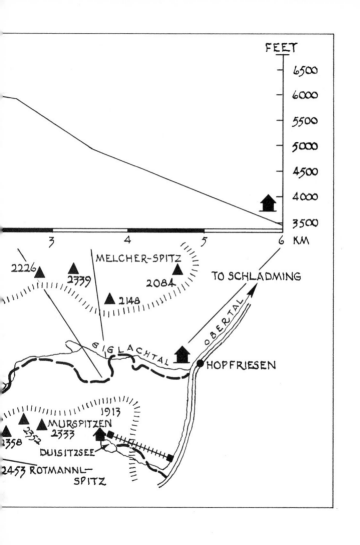

Obertal from Hopfriesen.

Giglach Brook, except for a section around Landauersee. It is a somewhat rougher trail than the one from Keinprecht and will take a little longer, although the distances are about the same.

From the hut, the trail leads northeastward along Unter Giglachsee to the outlet, which it crosses. At the trail junction here, the left branch leading down the valley is followed (the right branch is the trail to Rotmandlscharte). In about a half-kilometer, another trail junction is reached. The right fork leads to the tiny Duisitzsee and its privately operated (but open to the public) hut.

The left branch crosses the brook to the left bank, crosses a flat meadow, reaches Giglach-Alm and crosses back over to the right bank. After following the brook for about a half-kilometer, the trail swings slightly to the right, staying on the contour as the brook descends in a narrow ravine to Landauersee. After passing the small lake, the trail finally turns left and switchbacks to the brook at Lackner Alm. It then proceeds down to the valley, reaching Obertal Brook just above the Hopfriesen Inn.

The little inn at Hopfriesen is the terminus of a busline that runs through the Obertal to Schladming. Service is infrequent. There is one trip in the morning at about 0830 and one in the evening at 1700 (check the schedule). The fare is about 16 schillings and the trip takes half an hour. And it is quite a ride. At the upper end of the valley, the road is no wider than the bus, and I am sure that there are places where the trees brush both sides of the bus at the same time. But it beats walking. In Schladming, the terminus is the town square.

Time from Ignaz-Mattis Hut to Giglach Alm, ½ h; to Lackner Alm, 1½ h; to Hopfriesen, 2 h.

8. The Lechtaler Alps: a week in the heart of the Arlberg

The Inn River enters Austria near the common corner of Italy, Switzerland and Austria, flows north to Landeck, then turns abruptly east down the beautiful Inn Valley to Innsbruck. In this stretch, the valley is broad and green, dotted with farms and small villages. It forms a natural route to the west, to Switzerland. The Inn itself rises high in the Swiss Engadin. West from Landeck, a tributary valley, the Stanzertal, provides access to the Lechtaler Alps. This valley meets an obstacle in the high Arlberg Pass. Both the auto road that crosses the pass and the 10-kilometer long Arlberg tunnel were great engineering feats when they were built.

To many, the word "Arlberg" conjures up visions of Alpine skiing and the Arlberg techniques pioneered by Hannes Schneider. Indeed, some of the finest skiing in Austria is still to be found in St. Anton am Arlberg, and in Zurs and Lech nearby. These same mountains provide some of the most scenic and rewarding summertime hiking of any in Austria.

The Lechtaler Alps and the Lechquellengebirge (literally, the Lech-source mountains) are part of the limestone mountains that stretch in a great east-west band from the Swiss border nearly to Vienna. The rocks are light in color, and produce a sense of brightness and openness that is reminiscent of many parts of the Sierra Nevada, the "Range of Light." The limestone produces many interesting geological formations through which our route passes.

Access to the area is provided by the Arlberg railroad, which stretches from Innsbruck westward to Zurich. Service is frequent, and the express trains make the trip from Innsbruck to St. Anton or to Langen (at the western terminus of the Arlberg tunnel) in about two hours. From Zurich, the trip is about three hours, and for some it may be more convenient to fly to Zurich and board the eastbound train there. The route from Innsbruck is a spectacular one, following the Inn valley for much of the trip, between the Wettersteingebirge and the Lechtaler Alps on the north, and the Stubai, the Ötztal and Ferwall mountains on the south. Lech, the starting point for this walking trip, is a few miles north of the rail line, and can be reached by postal bus from St. Anton or Langen. The best service is from Langen, about every two hours. It is but a half-hour ride from either station, and the trip over the Flexen pass is a tortuous and spectacular one. For an avid skier, the choice is perhaps from Langen, for from this side, the bus passes through the little village of Stuben, the birthplace of Hannes Schneider.

Lech, at an elevation of 1450 meters, lies in a beautiful valley along the upper reaches of the Lech River. It is an old village, founded in the 13th century by immigrants from the Wallis district in Switzerland. The Walser church which dominates the main street dates from that early time. Since completion of the road over the Flexen pass at the beginning of the present century, Lech increasingly has become a favorite tourist spot. There are many inns, hotels and pensions; overnight accommodations are not difficult to obtain even during the height of the tourist season. There is a 55-bed youth hostel in Lech also. Information on accommodations may be obtained from the local tourist office, which is located on the east side of the main street near the base station of the Rufikopf cable car.

Since this district is very popular with hikers, August may find many of the huts in the area quite crowded. The best time is likely to be July, or early September.

Numerous maps and guidebooks are available for the area around Lech. Kompass Wanderkarte No. 33, *Arlberg Gebiet*, at a scale of 1:50,000, covers the complete route described, as does Freytag-Berndt Wanderkarte No. 37 *Bregenzer Wald*, at a scale of 1:100,000. The Alpenverein map 3/2, *Arlberg Gebiet*, covers most of the area at a scale of

Omeshorn over Lech.

1:25,000, but the adjoining map, 3/1, *Klostertaler Alpen*, is required to include the section around the Biberacher Hut. The federal survey Wanderkarten are especially good, but unfortunately, the route circles the common corner of four maps. To cover the entire route, these sheets are needed: Bezau, No. 112; Mittelberg, No. 113; Schruns, No. 142; and Sankt Anton am Arlberg, No. 143. Rudolf Rother also publishes a map and guidebook to the *Allgäuer und Lechtaler Alpen, Bregenzerwald und Lechquellengebirge*, Map No. 3. The maps, at a scale of 1:50,000 are supplemented by text in German that includes descriptions of the routes from hut to hut, and photographs showing main routes.

Rother also publishes the standard guidebook for the area, *Bregenzerwald und Lechquellengebirge*, by Walther Flaig. This also is in German, but will be useful if you can read it, especially if you contemplate climbing any of the peaks. A guidebook, mostly for tourists, *Summer guide to Lech-Oberlech, Zürs, Stubenbach and Zug am Arlberg*, by Günther Rinke, is available from the Lech tourist office. It is in German, English and French and describes the trails and easy climbs accessible from Lech. It has a useful photographic panorama of the mountains surrounding the village.

The choice of map for the hut-hopper lies

between the Kompass No. 33, and the F/B No. 36. Either will be quite adequate for the described trip.

The trip circles the headwaters of the Lech River, starting from the village and returning there after visiting four huts and one mountain inn. If desirable, after the last night at the Ravensburger Hut, the hiker may head directly for Langen, rather than walking to Lech and taking the postal bus to the railroad station. It is a beautiful circle tour that passes by several small reservoirs and lakes, and some of the most beautiful mountains in Austria, including the famous *Rote Wand* (Red Wall).

Lech.

From Lech to Körbersee

Körbersee is a small lake that sits in a depression above the village of Schröcken, high on the Hochtannberg Pass. A private hotel, the Körbersee, is located on the lake and has a commanding view of the Mohnenfluh (2542 m.), the Braunarl Spitz (2649 m.) and Hochberg (2323 m.). The latter two peaks lie on the ridge separating the Lech drainage from the Grosser Walsertal, a valley that opens to the west, joining the Rhine valley at the Swiss border. The hotel is accessible only by trail and is a favorite goal of hikers from Schröcken. There is a ski-lift that runs up from the hotel, so it is open

Hotel Körbersee in an August snowstorm.

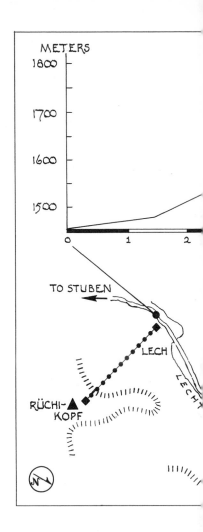

Lech to Körbersee

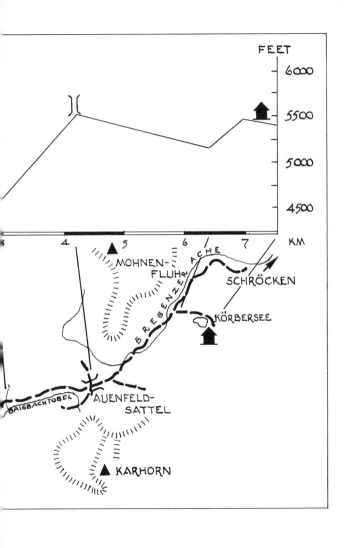

and busy in the wintertime as well. Rates are moderate, though, and it makes a fine stopping place for a hiker touring the Lech area.

The route from Lech follows the main road north toward Warth for about a kilometer. Here a side road branches left (sign) and slabs up the hillside. At a point where the road to Oberlech swings abruptly left, a path leads straight ahead to the north, following a narrow dirt road that is closed to traffic. The path follows around the end of a ridge, passes under the cable of the *Materialbahn* to Gaisbach Alm, crosses the Kitbach, and climbs upward along the left bank of the Gaisbachtobel, until it reaches the *Auenfeld Sattel* at 1709 meters (sign and trail junction).

The Auenfeld is a broad, high-mountain pasture that is the source of the Bregenz River. The trail from the pass continues northwesterly along the brook, crossing over it several times. At the end of the flat portion, just before the brook starts downward through a rocky cleft, a trail branches right (sign) to Körbersee. This climbs slightly, finally topping a ridge a hundred feet or so above the lake, then follows the west shore to the hotel.

Time from Lech to Auenfeld Sattel, 2 h; to trail junction, 3 h; to Körbersee, 3½ h.

Körbersee Hotel: 1660 meters. 120 beds, 20 *Matratzenlager*. Electricity, telephone: Schröcken (05-515-9365).

From Körbersee to Biberacher Hut

Schröcken is very nearly the archetype of the tiny Austrian mountain village. It is set in a narrow valley at the head of the Bregenzer Ache, just before the steep rise to Hochtannberg Pass. The village is dominated by an old and very picturesque church, and the few houses and inns cluster around it closely.

The trail from Körbersee to the village starts down toward the lake, but before reaching it, branches right (sign) and heads across the meadow and through patches of trees. (Another parallel route branches right at the south end of the lake. Both routes join the valley trail at the same point.) Descending slowly at first, the trail swings southward and descends more sharply, shortly joining the trail from Auenfeld Alm on the north side of the brook. Turning right (west), the trail follows the brook, but stays well above the narrow gorge, finally reaching Hochtannberg road at a switchback just above Schröcken. The road is followed down to the village, which is reached in about a half mile.

The route follows the road west through the village (supplies and lodging), past the even smaller village of Unterboden, and into a narrow valley. At the first brook entering from the left at Landsteg, a trail (sign) departs from the road to the left and descends to the Bregenzer Ache, crossing it on a bridge, and starts up the west (right) side of the

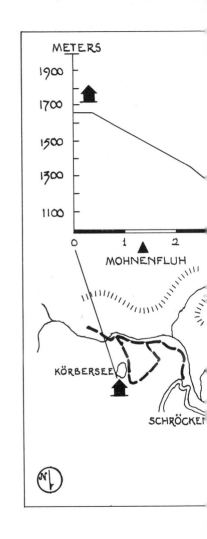

Körbersee to Biber-
acher Hut

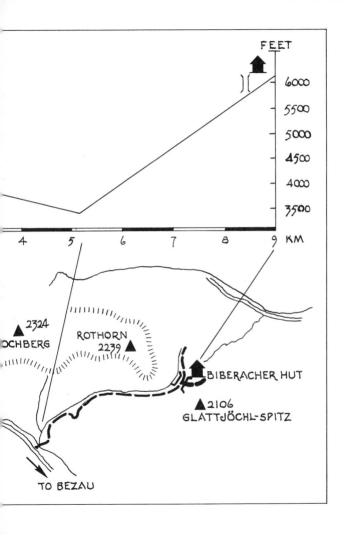

small tributary. The trail turns briefly away from the brook, then loops back and follows the general course of the valley to the southwest, staying on the northwest side of the brook. The trail here is broad and well-graded and is used as a stock drive. It is marked red-white-red.

At the top, at Schadonapass (1840 m.), the path crosses boggy meadows on a broad saddle. At the west end, at a sign, the trail forks left (south) and climbs in a hundred meters or so to the hut.

Biberacher Hut is smaller and older than many, but very comfortable and friendly. It is lighted by gaslight, but has running water. The main room has a most comfortable aspect. A fine old tile furnace sheds a warm glow over the room on a chilly day.

Time from Körbersee to Schröcken, 1 h; to Landsteg (start of trail to the hut), 1½ h; to Biberacher Hut, 4 h.

Biberacher Hut: 1846 meters. Built 1910. Open late June to early October. 10 beds, 42 *Matratzenlager*, 20 emergency beds.

From Biberacher Hut to Göppinger Hut

The trail between the two huts drops more than 400 meters, then climbs back twice that to the higher Göppinger Hut. Magnificent views of the Braunarl Spitze are to be had for much of the route; and the last portion traverses the wild and forbidding Gamsboden, a broad glacial cirque strewn with great boulders.

From the hut, the trail proceeds southward, then southeastward over the Schadona Alp and drops to a swampy depression, which it crosses. It then climbs gently to the Lite hut, a small barn, which it passes on the left. Shortly beyond, the trail forks, and the direct route to Göppinger Hut branches right (marked red/yellow).

(The left fork proceeds to the Fürggele, a pass on the north ridge of the Braunarl Spitze. An alternate route to Göppinger Hut traverses the summit, but it requires some rock climbing experience.)

Biberacher Hut.

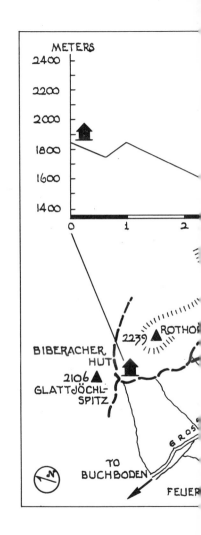

Biberacher Hut to
Göppinger Hut

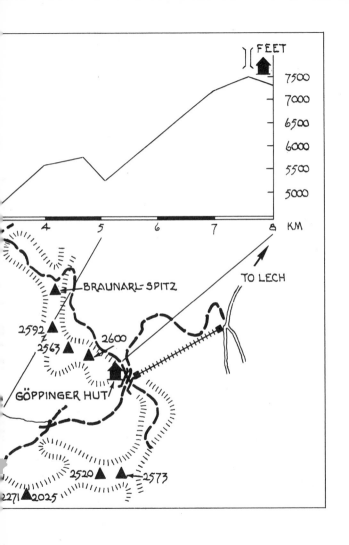

The trail proceeds down the Metzgertobel, crosses the brook, continues to slab downward (southwestward) until it crosses another brook (the Alpschelle Brook) where it meets a junction. Following the left branch, the trail climbs westward by switchbacks to just below the so-called Upper Alpschelle, then branches right and climbs to a barn. (The left branch is an old abandoned route. The right branch — painted with arrow and "G. H." on boulder — is the one to follow.) Near the building, the trail turns sharply left (west) and descends slightly, beneath a cliff, crosses a rough talus slope and swings south to a trail junction. The right branch ascends to the Mutterwang Joch. The route follows the right branch and ascends the limestone Bratschenwanne.

Göppinger Hut.

At the east end of the Bratschenwanne, the trail crosses over the ridge into the Gamsboden. It then climbs along the eastern edge of the Gamsboden to the pass, which is flat, and proceeds in a few minutes to Göppinger Hut.

Time from Biberacher Hut to lowest point (second brook crossing), 1 h; to Upper Alpschelle, 2 h; to Göppinger Hut, 4 h.

Göppinger Hut: 2245 meters. Built 1912; rebuilt and enlarged, 1967. Open mid-June to early October. 30 beds, 40 *Matratzenlager*, 15 emergency beds. Electricity, running water.

From Göppinger Hut to Freiburger Hut

This section is one of the most beautiful and rewarding portions of the entire route, crossing the upper end of the wild and forbidding Gamsboden, then traversing the great glacial cirque of the Johanneswanne and Johannes Pass with its majestic views of the Rote Wand. Although the walk takes only about four hours, the views are so numerous and worthy that extra time should be allowed for picture-taking and just enjoying the scenery.

From the hut, the trail leads southwestward across the upper end of the Gamsboden, climbing slightly to reach the Johanneskopf ridge. Turning west, it climbs this ridge a short way before entering the great basin of the Johanneswanne, a boulder-strewn cirque at the upper reaches of the

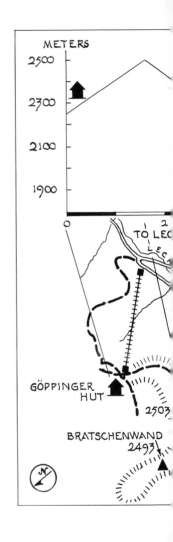

Göppinger Hut to
Freiburger Hut

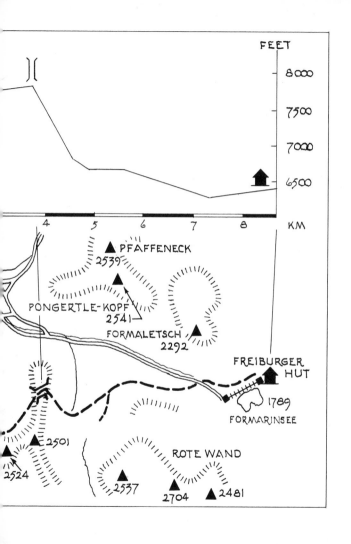

FEET

8000

7500

7000

6500

4   5   6   7   8   KM

PFAFFENECK
2539

PONGERTLE-KOPF
2541

FORMALETSCH
2292

FREIBURGER
HUT

1789
FORMARINSEE

2501

2524

ROTE WAND

2537   2704   2481

Johannes valley. The trail remains high on the wall, at about 2350 meters, eventually reaches the Johanneskanzel, the ridge stretching southeastward from the Hirschen Spitz, swings sharply to the right and starts the steep descent to Johannes Joch (2037 m.). The views of the Rote Wand (2704 m.) and the Rothorn (2357 m.) on the northeast ridge are magnificent all along this stretch from Johanneskanzel to Johannes Joch. Near the low point of the trail a small pond is visible to the left (south).

Crossing the Ober Gschröf, an interesting boulder-strewn field of light-colored limestone rocks characteristic of this region, the trail is joined by one entering from the right (sign). (This trail leads around the north flank of the Rote Wand to Klesenza Alp.)

Continuing straight ahead (south), the trail swings around the southeast slopes of Rote Wand, and slabs gently down to the road at Formarin Alp (1874 m.). The road is followed southwestward (up valley) a few yards to the parking lot at the end of the road. From here, the trail slabs the west slopes of a steep bluff above Formarin See, and climbs to Freiburger Hut (1918 m.). From the hut, the view north to Rote Wand over the reservoir below is spectacular, and justifiably makes Freiburger one of the most popular huts in the area. This is something of a warning, for its spectacular views and easy accessibility from the roadhead

Freiburger Hut.

mean that it is often crowded, especially during August, the height of the hiking season.

Time from Göppinger Hut to Johanneskepf ridge, 1 h; to Johanneskanzel, 2 h; to Johannes Joch, 2½ h; to trail junction, 2¾ h; to Formarin Alp, 3½ h; to Freiburger Hut, 4 h.

Freiburger Hut: 1918 meters. Built 1912. Open mid-June to mid-October. 16 beds, 50 *Matratzenlager* in main building; 18 *Matratzenlager* in auxiliary building. Electricity, running water, 2 common rooms.

From Freiburger Hut to Ravensburger Hut

If the previous day's journey was one of spectacular views, this day's trip is one of great geological, botanical and zoological interest. The route passes

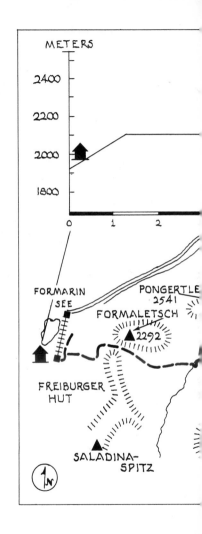

Freiburger Hut to
Ravensburger Hut

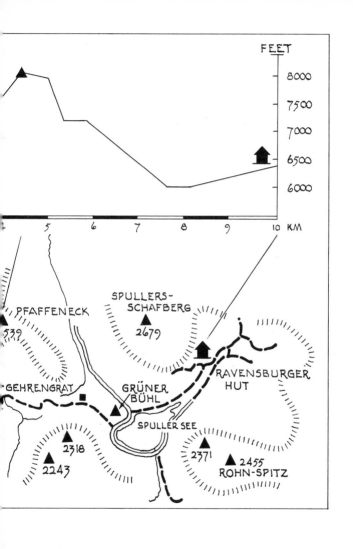

FEET

8000
7500
7000
6500
6000

4   5   6   7   8   9   10 KM

PFAFFENECK
539

SPULLERS-
SCHAFBERG
▲
2679

RAVENSBURGER
HUT

GEHRENGRAT

GRÜNER
BÜHL
▲

SPULLER SEE

▲
2318

▲
2243

▲
2371

▲ 2455
ROHN-SPITZ

through areas of heavily eroded limestone, with sinkholes and heavily creviced rocky flats. Marmots are common in the area, and the high meadows and swamps abound in colorful flowers. The multicolored limestone makes an extraordinary background for the flowers and curious geological formations. It is certainly one of the most rewarding sections of the tour.

The trail starts at the east end of Freiburger Hut (sign) and climbs eastward over grassy slopes, following a wide path. Reaching a small valley, the path swings left (north) and ascends around a broad shoulder, finally leveling out as it swings eastward again and reaches the broad saddle separating the Formaletsch on the north (2292 m.) and the Ganahls Kopf (2314 m.) on the south. At the east end of the broad saddle, the trail descends sharply to the *Steineres Meer*, a "stony sea" of curiously eroded limestone. The trail wanders through this region of boulders and crevices; care should be taken to stay on the marked way, for it is easy to become lost, especially in foggy weather.

At the east end of the limestone, the trail bends north (left) and follows a swampy brook (the Radonatobel), crosses to the right bank and starts the steep climb to the Gehrengrat. The trail switchbacks up the steep grassy slope, affording fine views of the deeply eroded and colorful region just traversed. After reaching the ridge, the trail

Rote Wand from Freiburger Hut.

proceeds southeastward over the broad, nearly flat ridge for about a half mile. At the end of the ridge, the trail bears left and starts the steep descent to the Dalaaser Schütz via numerous switchbacks.

At the bottom, the trail crosses a brook (the Glongtobel) and swings eastward in a slow descent to the bench above Spuller Brook. Here it passes to the right of the Schützalphütte after a short swing to the north, proceeding to and through the cleft between a small hill to the left, the Grüner Bühel, and the northeast slopes of the Plattnitzerjoch Spitz on the right. Spuller See is soon reached, and the trail meets the road around the reservoir. The shortest route is to the left, over the north-end dam, and on a graded and well-marked path, climbing to Ravensburger Hut along the left side of the main tributary brook.

Time from Freiburger Hut to saddle above Steineres Meer, 1 h; to Gehrengrat, 2½ h; to Spuller See, 4½ h; to Ravensburger Hut, 5 h.

Ravensburger Hut: 1948 meters. Built 1912, rebuilt 1959. Open mid-June to early October. 13 beds, 59 *Matratzenlager*, 20 emergency beds. Electricity, running water.

From Ravensburger Hut to Lech or Langen-am-Arlberg

To complete the circle, an easy trail proceeds over Stierloch Joch and drops down to the Lechtal and

Ravensburger Hut.

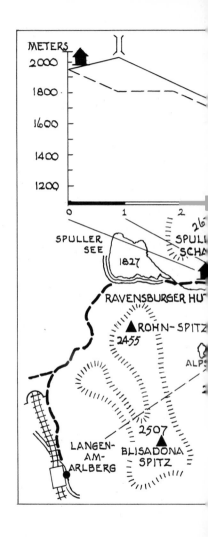

Ravensburger Hut
to Lech or Langen-
am-Arlberg

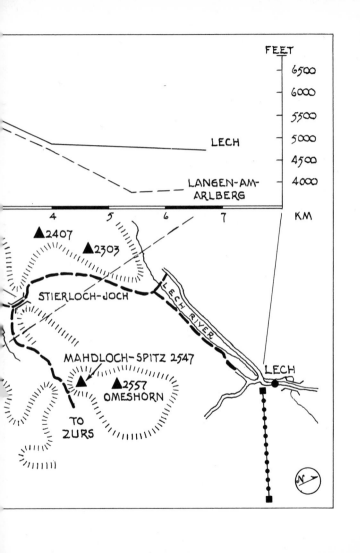

FEET

6500

6000

5500

5000 — LECH

4500

4000 — LANGEN-AM-
ARLBERG

4 5 6 7 KM

▲2407

▲2303

STIERLOCH-JOCH

LECH RIVER

MAHDLOCH-SPITZ 2547

▲ ▲2557
OMESHORN

TO
ZURS

LECH

N

thence to Lech. However, if it is more convenient, one may go directly to Langen from the hut by a good and well-marked trail. Indeed, it is possible to start the walking tour from Langen, staying overnight in Lech in one of the many inns or pensions. This requires that the portion between Langen and Ravensburger be backtracked, but it is a short section.

Toward Lech, the trail leads northeastward from the hut up the left side of the Spuller Valley, staying quite high above the brook, climbing only gently (the pass is less than 100 meters above the hut). Just before the pass is reached, a trail junction and sign indicate the route right (east) to Madloch Joch and Zurs. At the pass, the trail turns west (left) and crosses a rocky head before reaching the talus slope on the west side of Stierloch Alm. The trail swings around to the north and northeast, slabbing gently downward toward the Lech Valley, which it reaches at the tiny village of Zug. At the trail junction before reaching the Lech River, a trail leads right (east) toward Lech via Omesberg. This is an attractive walk through woods and fields. Alternatively, one can cross over to Zug and walk the road to Lech.

Time from Ravensburger Hut to Stierloch Joch, ½ h; to Zug, 2 h; to Lech, 2½ h.

For the direct route from the hut to Langen, the

Rothorn over Zug.

trail down to Spullersee is taken, crossing over the
inlet brook to the east side just above the inlet.
The road is followed around the east side of the
reservoir to the east end of the dam at the south
end of the lake (there are two dams, one on the
north side, one on the south). A trail starts down
from this point, following the left (east) bank of
the outlet brook on an abandoned road (apparently the one used when the dam was built). In a flat
meadow a trail junction is reached, the right
branch leading to the village of Wald. The left
branch leaves the brook and crosses a low pass (an
old building on the right) to a point from which a

magnificent view of the Klöstertal may be enjoyed. The trail swings left, following another brook, then swings south (right), staying on the right bank of the brook. In a short distance, it crosses over to the left bank on a bridge. After crossing a tributary brook, the trail to Langen diverges left. This junction is rather obscure, and should be watched for carefully. There is a sign on a tree above and to the left of the main path. (The main path leads to Klösterle, from which one must walk up the main road to Langen.) The path to Langen is much narrower and less used, but is easily followed. It descends through the woods, passing a number of avalanche protection structures. Just above Langen, the trail drops down to the railroad which is crossed over (watch for the trains) to reach the Arlberg highway. Follow the highway east under the railroad bridge to the station a few yards further on.

Time from Ravensburger Hut to Spullersee dam, ½ h; to Langen trail, 1½ h; to Langen railroad station, 2 h.

9. The Stubai Alps: a week in glacier country

Immediately to the southwest of Innsbruck stand the magnificent Stubai Alps. Elevations range from 600 meters at Innsbruck to just over 3500 meters at the summit at Zuckerhutl on the Italian border. Some of the highest peaks and largest glaciers in Austria are to be found here and in the neighboring Ötztal Alps immediately to the west. It is spectacular country with sharp granite peaks and ridges separated by glaciers that reach down to about 2500 meters.

The natural access route to the region is through the beautiful Stubai Valley, which branches southwestward from the Sill Valley a few kilometers south of Innsbruck. The Sill Valley stretches southward towards Brenner Pass, and separates the Stubai from the Tuxer Alps to the east. The Stubai has been lived in at least since 1,000 A.D., and dates its present name from that time.

The walking tour described in this chapter traverses a counterclockwise route from Neustift, about midway in the Stubai Valley, to Ranalt, at the head end. It skirts the lower end of several of the main glaciers, crosses several 2800 meter passes and affords the opportunity to climb several easy

Neustift.

peaks including one "three-thousander," the
Rinnenspitz near Franz Senn Hut. It is the highest
route of the three described in this book and is the
most demanding physically, but also perhaps the
most rewarding visually. It is the only one of the
three that is in the heart of the glacier country.

One portion of the walk crosses the lower end of
the Hochmoos Glacier above the New Regensburger Hut. It is not a particularly dangerous crossing, however, and does not require that the party
be roped for safety. Neither crampons nor ice-ax
are necessary, although four-point instep crampons
(*Vierzacker*) may be useful on one short stretch.

Starting point for the trip is at Neustift, the
terminus of the bus route from Innsbruck. (Service
at about two hour intervals starts from the plaza at
the south end of the Innsbruck *Hauptbahnhof*.
One-way fare is about 8 schillings; a pack too large
to be carried on your lap will cost an extra 4 schillings). The walk may be started at the end of the
bus ride in the main square of Neustift, or a jeep
ride may be taken from there to Oberiss, at the
very end of the road in the Oberberg Valley. The
Land Rovers that are used can be seen at the east
side of the main square, with signs indicating their
destination. The trip to Oberiss Alm costs about 30
schillings, and may be worth it. However, the walk
up Oberberg Valley along Alpeiner Brook is a
pretty one, and you will see more of the country-

side that way. It is a long walk, and if the hour is late, it may be better to take the jeep ride.

The best time of year for this trip is probably July or September. The weather is usually better in August, but the huts tend to be more crowded then. June may find some of the trails with much snow, but there should be no trouble late in the month.

The Alpenverein publishes an up-to-date pair of maps covering the Stubai. Sheet 31/1 (*Hochstubai, Südblatt*) at a scale of 1:25,000 covers the described route except for the first part from Neustift to Franz Senn Hut. Sheet 36, *Innsbruck-Brenner*, of the Kompass Wanderkarte series, covers the entire area at a scale of 1:50,000. Freytag-Berndt publishes a 1:100,000 map of the *Stubaier Alpen*, No. 24 of their series. Two sheets of the Austrian federal survey cover the area: No. 147 (*Axams*) on the west, and No. 148 (*Brenner*) on the east. And lastly, Rudolf Rother Bergverlag in Munich publishes a sectional map of the Stubai and Ötztaler Alps at a scale of 1:50,000 – their Map 5. This also contains photographs, and German text.

Several German-language guidebooks are available, published by Rudolf Rother in Munich. The *Stubaier Alpen Kleiner Führer* has 112 pages of information on trails and climbs in the area, and includes a 1:50,000 scale full-color map. It has a number of photographs including two panoramas which help greatly in identifying the peaks. Rother also publishes a larger edition by W. Rabensteiner and H.E. Klier, the *AV-Führer Stubaier Alpen*. The smaller volume costs about two dollars, the larger about six dollars. Yet another guidebook, *Wagner's Wanderbuch durch das Stubaier Tal*, is published by *Wagner's Universität Buchhandlung* in Innsbruck.

With all these maps and guides available, what to choose? The Rother *Kleiner Führer* contains a good map for the hut-hopper as well as photos and other information on huts and trails. Much of this is useful even if your German is extremely limited. Furthermore, the map is the only one at the scale of 1:50,000 that covers the entire route on one sheet.

The described trip from Neustift to Ranalt can be done in five days and four nights without pushing too hard. However, counting on a day or two for side trips and the possibility of weather delays, a full week can profitably be allotted to the trip.

From Neustift to Franz Senn Hut

A few yards west of the bus-stop in the town square of Neustift, a sign indicates the road to Oberberg. After you follow this road for about ten minutes, a trail takes off to the right (sign), following the base of the slope on the north side of

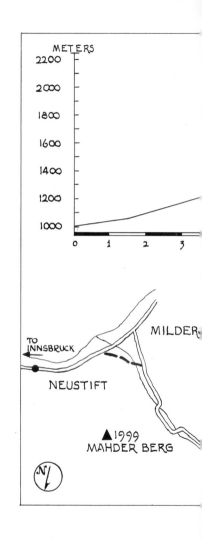

METERS

2200
2000
1800
1600
1400
1200
1000

0   1   2   3

MILDER

TO
INNSBRUCK

NEUSTIFT

▲1999
MAHDER BERG

Neustift to Franz
Senn Hut

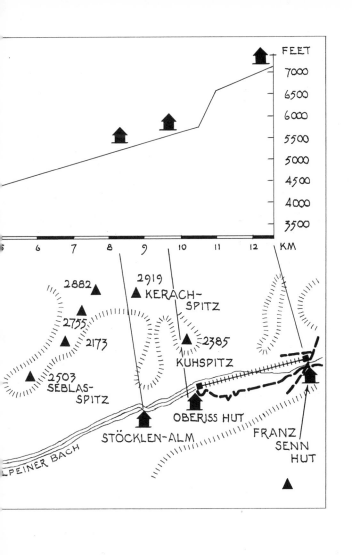

FEET
7000
6500
6000
5500
5000
4500
4000
3500

6 7 8 9 10 11 12 KM

2882 ▲
2919 ▲ KERACH-
SPITZ
2755 ▲
2173 ▲
▲ 2385
KUHSPITZ
2503 ▲
SEBLAS-
SPITZ
OBERISS HUT
STÖCKLEN-ALM
FRANZ
SENN
HUT
ALPEINER BACH
▲

Oberiss Hut above the Oberbergtal.

Alpeiner Brook. In about a mile, the trail crosses to the south bank over a bridge and continues westward following a narrow road. In about three and a half miles, the road crosses back over to the north side at Stöckeln Alm (refreshments) and climbs steeply for three-fourths of a mile to Oberiss Hut, the end of the gravel track and the beginning of the trail to Franz Senn Hut. The *Materialbahn* servicing Franz Senn Hut terminates here. One may have his pack carried to the hut via this tramway for a charge of about 10 schillings. The pack will be waiting when the hiker arrives at the hut.

From Oberiss, the trail leads westward across a

meadow and then climbs sharply on a series of switchbacks, staying to the north side of the brook. (Just below the switchbacks, avoid paths to the left that dead-end at the brook.) After a climb of about a mile, the way becomes less steep, and the hut shortly comes into view. Views are extensive on this stretch, which is above timberline. The trail is marked with red and white paint, stripes below Oberiss, circles above.

Franz Senn Hut is located in view of the Alpeiner Glacier at an elevation of 2150 meters. It is a large hut, really a hotel, with accommodations for more than 250 people. Although somewhat

Franz Senn Hut.

more expensive than average (bed with sheets and blankets costs $1.50 for Alpine Club members; dinner with wine about $2.00), it is very comfortable and well equipped.

A number of peaks are accessible from Franz Senn Hut. These include the Schrankogel, Fernerkogel, Villerspitze, Ruderhofspitze, Schrandele; and the Rinnenspitz, which is described next. Guides are available at the hut if you wish to climb one of the more difficult peaks.

Time from Neustift to Oberiss, 4 h.; to Franz Senn Hut: 5½ h.

Franz Senn Hut: 2147 meters. Open 1 June to 15 October. 158 beds, 86 bunk spaces, 20 emergency beds. Electricity, flush toilets, hot showers, drying room. Jeep transportation available from Neustift to Oberiss. Telephone 05-226-218.

Franz Senn Hut to the Rinnenspitz and return

Although the Rinnenspitz is a relatively minor peak on the ridge separating the Lisenser Glacier from the Alpeiner Glacier, it affords spectacular views of the highest peaks and glaciers in the Stubai region. It is just over three thousand meters in height (3003, to be exact), and it is easily climbed by a good, marked trail. It also presents the opportunity for attaining at least one "three-thousander" — certainly the best peak in the area of Franz Senn Hut that can be climbed by one

Habicht from the Rinnenspitz.

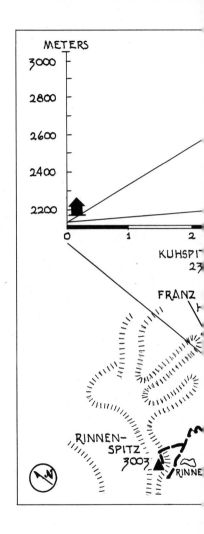

Franz Senn Hut to Rinnenspitz and to New Regensburger Hut

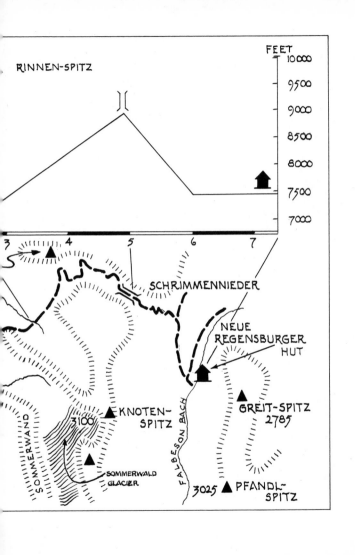

Sommerwand from near the summit of Rinnenspitz.

without rock-climbing or glacier-crossing experience.

The trail from the hut leads northward over a bridge, bears sharply right, and leads in about ten minutes to a trail junction. The trail angles sharply to the left, following the sign to the Rinnen See, and slabs the valley wall in a southwesterly direction. In a short while a flat bench is reached and the outlet of the Rinnen See is crossed. The trail then climbs more sharply to another trail junction, just below the lake, which, though not yet visible, can be reached in five minutes. The lake is a glacial tarn set in a cirque reminiscent of many of the small high-altitude lakes of the Sierra.

From the junction, the trail to the peak branches northward (sign) and climbs the southeast ridge in a series of switchbacks. The peak is clearly visible from this stretch. The summit ridge is attained about 200 meters east of the summit. Although the ridge is sharp and rocky, the way is clearly marked. Some rock scrambling is required and in a few places cables are placed to assist the climber. *Trittsicherheit*, a secure step, is required on this stretch, but the scramble is not difficult. Peaks and glaciers in profusion are visible in all directions.

Total time for the climb is about 3 h; to Rinnen See, about 2 h. Return journey, about 1½ h.

From Franz Senn Hut to New Regensburger Hut

The route to the New Regensburger Hut, the Franz Hörtnagel Way, traverses the Schrimmennieder, a high pass (2706 meters), between Oberbergtal on the north and Falbeson Brook, a tributary of Unterbergtal, on the south. The entire way is above timberline, and affords fine views of the two valleys and the surrounding ridges.

The path leads eastward from Franz Senn Hut (sign) and slabs the north ridge of the Gschwezgrat, climbing gently. Rounding the ridge, the trail turns southeastward and crosses the Kuhgschwez (Kuh-

New Regensburger Hut.

g'schwez), a broad glacial valley that is used extensively for grazing. After crossing several small tributaries of Alpeiner Brook, the trail turns south and climbs the Platzengrube by a series of long switchbacks, keeping to the east side of the valley. The final climb to Schrimmennieder is a long steep traverse of the talus slope. The ridge is actually traversed just to the east of the lowest point, at an elevation of 2745 meters.

The trail leads straight down the talus on the south side of the pass for about a hundred yards, then turns left and works its way down the talus in a series of switchbacks, reaching a trail junction at 2300 meters. The trail to New Regensburger Hut (sign) branches right and follows the contour for about a mile to the hut.

The hut is located at the lower (east) end of the Hohes Moos, a mossy meadow through which Falbeson Brook flows. Above lies the Hochmoos Glacier; below, Falbeson Brook cascades steeply down to the Alm below. The glacier-covered Ruderhof Spitz (3473 meters) dominates the view up the valley. The hut has been recently remodeled and is most comfortable.

Time from Franz Senn Hut: 4 h. Route marked in red and white.

New Regensburger Hut: 2286 meters. Built 1931, rebuilt 1966/67. Open 15 June to 30 September. 10 beds, 65 *Matratzenlager*, 5 emergency

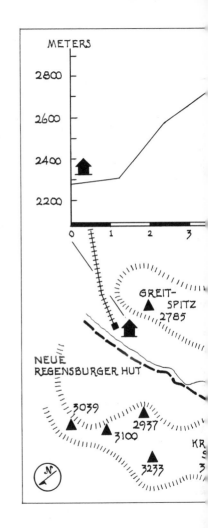

New Regensburger
Hut to Dresdner
Hut

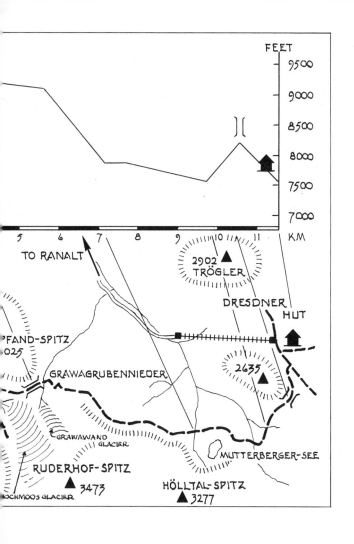

FEET

9500

9000

8500

8000

7500

7000

5   6   7   8   9   10   11   KM

TO RANALT

2902
TRÖGLER

DRESDNER
HUT

PFAND-SPITZ
3025

GRAWAGRUBENNIEDER

2635

GRAWAWAND
GLACIER

MUTTERBERGER-SEE

RUDERHOF-SPITZ

3473

HÖLLTAL-SPITZ
3277

HOCHMOOS GLACIER

Dresdner Hut.

beds. Telephone.

From New Regensburger Hut to Dresdner Hut

The route to Dresdner Hut is long and somewhat arduous, but scenically rewarding. It is the only leg of the trip that crosses a glacier. Although not a dangerous crossing, the way may be obscured in fog or bad weather and should be attempted only when visibility is good.

From New Regensburger Hut, the trail leads west up the beautiful Hohes Moos, a flat swampy meadow fed by drainage from the Hochmoos Glacier. The trail gradually climbs the right side of the valley until it reaches a trail junction just below the tiny mountain tarn, the Falbesoner See (2577 m.). (The trail right leads in a few yards to the lake.) From the junction, the trail turns southward across the rock-strewn tongue of the Hochmoos Glacier, and is marked by red and white stripes on the rocks. However, the path across the hard ice is indistinct and could be obscured in a dense fog. The Grawagrubennieder, the low point in the ridge directly opposite, is clearly visible from this point, and the way leads directly toward it, finally climbing a steep snowfield set against the ridge. Footing is somewhat precarious at the top end of the snowfield and four-point crampons are useful if not absolutely necessary. At a point marked by a large red and white dot on a large boulder, the trail starts the steep and rocky climb to the pass. (Use care so as to not dislodge loose rocks that may endanger hikers below.)

At the top of the pass (2880 m.) a fine view of the major Stubai peaks on the Italian border can be seen. The path now heads generally southwesterly, toward Mutterberg See, slabbing the south slopes of the Ruderhof Spitz, losing elevation except for short climbs over several minor ridges. Just below Mutterberg See, which has been visible for most of the way from the pass, several small glacial ponds are passed. Continuing downward and turning more to the south, the trail reaches the low point of this section (2280 m.) and one of the streams draining the Daunkogel Glacier is crossed on a bridge.

The trail now climbs sharply to Egesen Joch (2506 m.). In a few yards, Dresdner Hut comes into view, and the trail descends sharply to it.

Dresdner Hut is a capacious hostel, one of the largest in the area. The accommodations are fine, although somewhat more expensive than some of the other huts. It is used in the late winter and spring for skiing, and a ski lift is being constructed nearby.

Time from New Regensburger Hut to Grawa-grubennieder, 2½ h (red and white markings); to bridge at stream crossing, 5 h (red and white, then white only); to Egesen Pass, 6 h (red and white); to Dresdner Hut, 6½ h (red and white).

Dresdner Hut: 2302 m. Open 15 February to 15 October. 80 beds, 120 *Matratzenlager*, 50 emergency spaces. Electricity. Telephone, Neustift 05-226-213.

From Dresdner Hut to Sulzenau Hut

The easiest way from Dresdner Hut to Sulzenau Hut is over Peil Joch. Somewhat more difficult, but many times more rewarding, is the route that traverses the Grosser and Kleiner Trögler, two peaks directly on line between the two huts. The way is well marked, and the view from the summits spectacular.

Both routes start out from Dresdner Hut on the same trail, which leads eastward, crossing the outlet of Schaufel and Fernau glaciers, then climbing steeply toward Peil Joch. In about half an hour, the routes divide, the easier path over the pass branching to the right and climbing over rocky slopes to the pass. The path up the Trögler continues eastward, climbing up steep talus slopes to the ridge, and thence in a few yards to the summit of the Grosser Trögler (2902 m.). A large cross and a surveyor's triangulation tripod have been erected

Ruderhofspitz from Gyünausee.

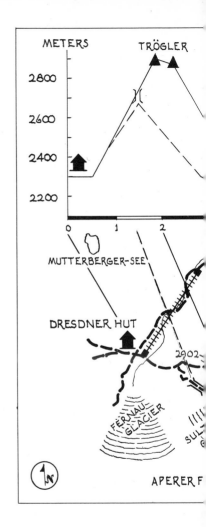

Dresdner Hut to
Sulzenau Hut and
Nürnberger Hut

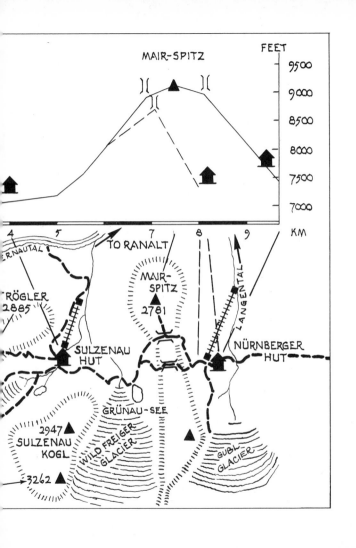

on the summit. (It should be noted here that it is a serious offense to tamper with government triangulation markers.)

The view from the summit is exceptional. To the south, the rounded dome of the Zuckerhütl (3503 m.) dominates the massive Sulzenau Glacier. To the left, the smaller Fernerstube joins the Sulzenau Glacier just at the foot of the Trögler. To the left of the Fernerstube rises the massive Wilder Freiger (3418 m.). To the northeast, the face of Habicht (3277 m.) with its two small glaciers appears. And to the north, the snow-covered face of the Ruderhof Spitz (3473 m.) dominates the view, just left of the ridge crossed by the trail from New Regensburger Hut.

Sulzenau Hut.

From the summit, the trail leads over the narrow ridge to the Kleiner Trögler (2885 m.) before starting the descent to the Sulzenau Hut. The trail here is steep and narrow and demands caution. After a series of switchbacks down the east slopes of the ridge, the trail crosses several lateral moraines of the Sulzenau Glacier, and reaches a trail junction near the brook. The left fork leads in a few minutes to the hut. The hut sits at the end of a hanging valley in a beautiful alpine setting, surrounded by rugged peaks, glaciers, snowfields and high alpine meadows.

Time from Dresdner Hut to Trögler summit, 2½ h; to Sulzenau Hut, 4h. Via Peil Joch, about ¾ h shorter.

Sulzenau Hut. 2191 meters. Built 1926, rebuilt 1959. Open middle of June to end of September. 30 beds, 57 *Matratzenlager*, 30 emergency spaces. Electricity.

From Sulzenau Hut to Nürnberger Hut

The route to Nürnberger Hut affords another rewarding climb over a minor peak — one that has spectacular views of the Stubai Alps and glaciers. As in the last section, the route offers two trails, the lower over the Niederl, a 2680-meter pass, the higher via the Mair Spitz, a 2781-meter peak. Both trails are good; the way is steep but not difficult.

The trail from Sulzenau Hut leads eastward

Hut-hoppers at Grünau See.

across the brook draining the Sulzenau Glacier,
curves northward and climbs gently to the beautiful Grünau See (2330 m.). This is certainly one of
the most beautiful mountain tarns in the Stubai, a
deep turquoise glacial lake formed by an abandoned lateral moraine of the Wild-Freiger Glacier.
High above the little lake towers the snow-covered
summit of the Wilder Freiger (3418 m.). On a
sunny day, the dazzling white snowfields and the
dark gray rocks contrast spectacularly with the turquoise of the lake and the lush green of the surrounding meadow grass.

At the north end of the lake, the trail forks
(sign). The left-hand fork leads northward and
climbs steeply for about a half mile to another

Sulzenau Glacier and Hut from Mair Spitz.

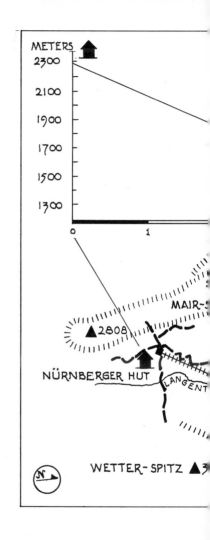

METERS

2300

2100

1900

1700

1500

1300

0   1

MAIR-

▲2808

NÜRNBERGER HUT

LANGENT

WETTER-SPITZ ▲3

Nürnberger Hut to
Ranalt

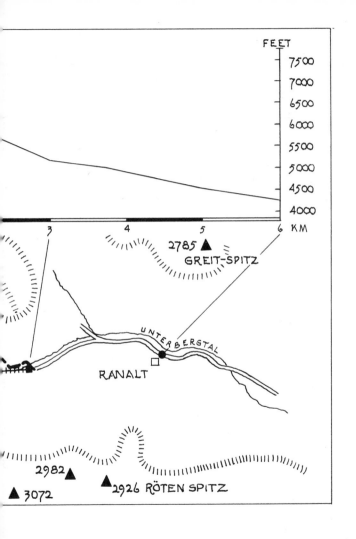

FEET

7500
7000
6500
6000
5500
5000
4500
4000

3 4 5 6 KM

2785 ▲
GREIT-SPITZ

UNTERBERGTAL

RANALT

2982 ▲ ▲ 2926 RÖTEN SPITZ

▲ 3072

Nürnberger Hut.

junction. The right-hand fork ascends to a low point on the ridge, the Niederl, then descends via switchbacks to Nürnberger Hut. The left branch, that to Mair Spitz, leads northward to the Schafgrubl, a rocky meadow with several shallow mountain lakes. The contrast between the crystal clear water of these spring-fed lakes and the turbid glacial water of the Grünau See is vivid. Passing the lakes, the trail switchbacks up the increasingly steep flank of the ridge, reaching the crest about a quarter mile from the summit. The trail forks at the ridge, the left fork proceeding north up the ridge to the summit. The last hundred yards or so are steep and rocky and require some rock-scrambling. The view from a flat grassy knoll just before the main summit is very nearly as good as from the top.

To reach Nürnberger Hut, the trail along the ridge must be retraced to the junction. Heading eastward, it crosses several rocky minor ridges before heading down to the hut via a series of switchbacks. Near the bottom, the trail over the Niederl is rejoined, and in a few hundred yards the hut is reached.

Time from Sulzenau Hut to Grünau See, 1 h; to Mair Spitz, 2 h; to Nürnberger Hut, 3 h.

Nürnberger Hut. 2280 meters. Open 15 June to 20 September. 62 beds, 106 *Matratzenlager*. Electricity.

From Nürnberger Hut to Ranalt and Innsbruck

Nürnberger Hut sits on a rocky ledge on the west side of the Langental. It is a popular hut that provides access to the Wilder Freiger, Feuerstein, and other peaks along the Italian border, and is only a three-hour climb from the bus station in Ranalt. An hour of this may be saved by taking the jeep from Ranalt to the end of the gravel road in Besuch Alm.

The trail to Ranalt from the hut is graded and well-worn. As a matter of fact, it is negotiable on crutches: I saw a one-legged man reach the hut, apparently without difficulty. The trail leads north from the hut, down the west side of the Langental, and zig-zags its way down to Besuch Alm, a pretty mountain pasture at an elevation of 1700 meters. The supplies cableway to the hut is located here, at the end of the road. From here, the trail follows the gravel road down the east side of Langental, through a Norway spruce forest, joining the road in Unterbergtal about a kilometer south of Ranalt.

The bus station in Ranalt is at the Falbesoner Gasthof, on the upper road at the north end of the village. Service is approximately every one-and-a-half or two hours in the summer season, and ter-

Bus stop in Ranalt.

minates in Neustift, where the bus to Innsbruck can be taken. The bus schedules are posted in most of the huts, and should be checked for the connection at Neustift. The trip from Ranalt to Neustift is about 40 minutes, and from Neustift to Innsbruck about an hour. The fares are 20 and 28 schillings, respectively.

Time from Nürnberger Hut to Besuch Alm, 1 h; to Ranalt, 2 h.

Appendix I/General hut regulations of the Alpine Clubs

Following is a translation (my own; not an authorized translation) of the Alpenverein hut regulations governing the huts operated by the Austrian and German Alpine Clubs. Huts operated by other organizations will have similar regulations. They are always posted in a conspicuous place in the hut.

GENERAL HUT REGULATIONS OF THE ALPINE CLUBS

I. Registration requirements and identification.

1. Each hut visitor must upon arrival in the hut sign the hut register and show his membership card on demand to the Section official or the hut manager. He must obey the local registration requirements. In case of refusal, his stay in the hut can be denied.

2. In order to make it easier to locate him in case of an accident or being lost, each visitor should enter in the hut record book the next destination in his mountain trip.

3. Hut privileges are granted only to those who can produce valid identification.

II. Claim to sleeping accommodations.

1. Members have the right of accommodations before non-members. Members who are on mountain trips have priority, adults before youths. Members are assigned sleeping places as available and as desired, immediately after their arrival, and have priority on beds.

2. Non-members are assigned beds after a time determined by the Section, but not before 19 hours (7 p.m.).

3. The allocation of sleeping places follows the order of entry in the hut register.

4. Privileged claim to a sleeping place before all hut visitors belongs to:

a) the sick or injured whose descent or transportation to the valley cannot be expected

b) mountain rescue personnel on duty

5. The following have claim to beds or mattresses:

a) Alpine Club members

b) Members of all those clubs with which reciprocal agreements exist

c) Wives of members of the German Alpine Club with valid identifications

d) Children of members according to a) and b) with Child-identification, accompanied by a parent

e) Members of Alpine Club Youth Groups or the youth group of a club as in b), accompanied by an adult who must be a member according to a) or b)

f) Children or youths in the company of an adult, responsible, card-carrying member. In this case, at most two visitors are allowed per member.

6. Youth groups as in 5a or 5b have claim only to mattress accommodations.

7. Claim to emergency accommodations can be made only when all beds and mattresses are reserved.

8. The hut manager is permitted to accept advance reservations only for members, but for no more than half of each type of accommodation to be found in the hut. Advance reservations for nonmembers is not permitted.

9. In case of a shortage of accommodations, only members who are engaged in a mountain tour, or who must remain in the hut for scientific purposes, are permitted to stay more than one night.

10. It is forbidden to place the hut at the disposal of groups which are not from the German or Austrian Alpine Clubs, or which were not arranged for by the Section, or for other private groups. Exceptions permitted to the management are approved only if the Section owning the hut has given its permission, and

a) the course leader is a member and his Section warrants his qualifications as course leader, or the course leader is an authorized mountain- or ski-guide;

b) at the most half of each type of accommodation is reserved.

11. Unmanaged and uncontrolled huts are open only to members, or non-members accompanying members.

III. Hut fees

1. Hut fees must lie within the established range.

2. Hut fees are collected in advance against delivery of an official receipt. Services are rendered only upon showing a valid identification.

3. A. All non-members pay full fees. Exceptions are given in a special list in the appendix.

B. Reduced member fees are paid by:

a) Alpine Club members and equivalents (II 5a and b);

b) Children of members and wives of members of the German Alpine Club with identification card when using beds;

c) Youth-group members (II 5e) when using beds;

d) Seriously injured veterans of both World Wars with greater than 50% disability.

C. Youth fees are paid only for mattresses by:

a) Members of the Alpine Club youth teams and equivalent groups;

b) Alpine Club youth groups and such equivalent clubs with a leader (II 6);

c) Children of members and Alpine Club youth group members and such equivalent clubs in company of a parent or an adult member (II 5d, e, f).

D. Those admitted without fee include service personnel, licensed mountain guides, apprentice guides, porters, members of the Mountain Rescue Service and mountain guards with written orders, members of the border- and security-service when on rescue missions, as well as officials who are working with the hut surveillance and patrol.

E. Day fees (trail and hut contributions) for those not staying overnight are paid by:

a) all non-members according to 3A;

b) all members and equivalent according to 3B.

F. All hut visitors except those exempted by D have to pay the Mountain Rescue fee in Austria. In Germany, non-members staying overnight pay the Mountain Guard fee.

G. All overnight visitors with the exception of those named in 3D pay the established baggage insurance premium in addition to the overnight fee. The hut manager is obliged to collect this premium. Liability limitations for personal belongings brought by overnight guests or over the custody of items checked by day visitors are given by the hut manager in an official notice.

H. Other fees.

Heating fees for central heat in bedrooms, fees for firewood, for cooking privileges, public taxes and so forth are paid by all hut guests at the same rate. No fee can be charged for heating the common room of a managed hut.

4. "Doubling-up" in sleeping places is permitted only in the case of overcrowding and only with consent of the hut manager. He can order doubling-up in the mattress room. In such cases, the various fees are reduced by a third.

5. Emergency facilities [*Notlager*] are simpler than those previously enumerated. Emergency facilities can only be claimed when the mattress room [*Matratzenlager*] is fully occupied. The establishment of permanent space which is rented cheaper than the mattresses is left to the choice of the Section. The charge for emergency space (*Notlager*) ought to be about half the charge for mattresses (*Matratzenlager*).

6. No kind of reduced fees or privileges of any type can be granted to members of the Section operating the hut over and above the other Alpine Club members.

7. A service charge of 10 percent is added to the overnight charges.

IV. Food Service

1. Food service in managed huts is to be established for the needs of the mountain climber (*Bergsteiger*).

2. A *Bergsteigerverpflegung* (mountain-climber provisions) as well as an inexpensive soft drink and tea water must be provided at all times according to the regulations of the Hut Committee. *Bergsteigeressen* (the special meal for mountain climbers) may also be served to non-members, but at a higher price. This special meal is listed at the top of the menu.

3. Each visitor is entitled to consume his own provisions, without losing the right of eligibility for sleeping accommodations and other services.

4. Where self-service facilities and particularly cooking facilities for self-service use by members are lacking, the use of a cooking facility must be made available, unless the hut manager can provide for the preparation at a suitable time of simple foods brought (by the member). Cooking and eating utensils should be made available to the members.

5. For the utilization and cleaning of utensils, for fuel, or for the preparation of food, moderate fees are established and posted by the Section.

6. Whether and in what way regulations 4 and 5 apply to visitors who are not members is established by the Section.

V. Rescue arrangements

1. The hut is to provide through the Section, according to the determination of the Executive Committee, rescue equipment which is to be reserved exclusively for Alpine disasters and cases of mountain emergencies. In each hut is a status list in a visible place of the rescue equipment available there, with the location of the nearest place to report Alpine disasters, the nearest rescue office, and the location of a doctor, as well as a medical report record.

2. Rescue equipment and a first aid kit are to be securely stored and kept complete. The hut manager is responsible for this. The use of these objects is permitted only for rescue operations.

3. In addition, the hut manager ought to provide a simple first-aid supply, which he can supply to the hut visitor in urgent cases for the replacement cost.

4. A first-aid textbook is to be provided with the rescue equipment through the Section.

VI. House rules

1. Decorum and custom are not to be violated in the huts and their environs. Violators can be ejected from the huts.

2. Absolute quiet prevails in the huts from 22 hours (10 p.m.). Also, early risers must behave in such a manner that quiet hours are not disturbed.

3. Those arriving after 22 hours [10 p.m.] have in general no further claim to food service.

4. Mechanical music instruments, musical and other presentations for pay are forbidden.

5. Radio reception is permitted. Receivers are permitted to be operated only in the hut manager's room. Only the hut manager is permitted to operate the radio, and only so long as it does not disturb anyone.

6. Radios or mechanical musical instruments brought by visitors are not permitted to be used either in the huts or in the vicinity.

7. The hut library is to be taken care of in the mountain-climber spirit.

8. Cooking and smoking in sleeping rooms is forbidden.

9. Reservation of seats in the common rooms is forbidden. In case of a shortage of seats, the hut manager can request the quick clearing of table-places.

10. Dogs are on principle not permitted in the kitchen or in sleeping rooms.

11. The perpetrator is responsible for each mischievous or negligent damage to the hut or its furnishings. Shoes are not to be worn in bed or on mattresses. The area around the hut is to be kept clean.

12. Advertising is not permitted in the vicinity of the huts.

13. The enforcement of house rules is the obligation of the hut manager, or his deputy, or ultimately, an Alpine Club deputy. Over this stands the supervisory duty of the Executive Committee.

14. The Executive Committee can grant exceptions to hut rules and tariffs. The exception is to be given in writing.

15. Complaints which cannot be resolved at the time and place are brought to the Section hut committee.

16. Those who do not observe the hut regulations can be banished from the huts and are liable for damage caused.

17. These hut regulations were adopted at the General Meeting of 1 December 1954.

Appendix II/Hut fee structure

Hut fees are posted in a conspicuous place. They are usually indicated on a standard poster, in schillings and groschen. Note that fees for non-members (*Nichtmitglieder*) are listed in a separate column. The column of members' fees also includes a list of other Alpine Clubs, members of which are entitled to the members' fees. Following is a translation of the items listed on the card:

1. *Bett mit Wäsche*	Bed with sheets and pillowcase
2. *Matratzenlager*	Bunk (blankets, no sheets)
3. *Wäsche für Matratzenlager (je Leintuch oder Wäscheschlafsack)*	Linen for bunk (one sheet or washable sleeping sack)
4. *Notlager*	Emergency bunk or space
5. *Weg- und Hüttengroschen (entfällt bei bezahlter Nächtigung)*	Trail-and hut-fee (omitted for paying overnight guests)
6. *Reisegepäckversicherung*	Baggage insurance

7. *Bergrettungs-* *groschen*	Mountain rescue fee
8. *Fremdenabgabe* *nach Landes-* *gesetz*	Tax for foreigners according to the law of the land
9. *Heizgebühren —* *für alle Hütten-* *besucher gleich!*	Heating fee — the same for all visitors!
im Gastraum — *keine*	in the common room — none.
im Schlafräumen *mit Zentralheizung*	in sleeping rooms with central heating
im Schlafräumen *mit Ofenheizung*	in sleeping rooms with heaters

"Notlager" is a simple space (as with the *Matratzenlager*) with one blanket; if no blanket is furnished, no overnight fee is charged, although the trail and hut fees (item 5) are charged. "Doubling-up" and the resulting fees charged are regulated by General Hut Regulation III 4.

A service charge of 10% is added to overnight fees (Items 1 through 4).

Overnight fees are paid daily and always in advance. Always ask for and keep the receipt. The hut manager is required to make a daily accounting.

Each visitor is required to sign the hut register.

If he does not he can be required to surrender his membership card or other pass before a sleeping space is allocated.

The "General Hut Regulations of the Alpine Clubs" regulate privileges and favors.

All inquiries, suggestions and complaints are referred to the appropriate Section.

Bibliography

Geology

Oxburgh, E.R. 1968. The geology of the eastern Alps. London: The Geologists Association. 127 pp.

Vegetation

Huxley, Anthony. 1967. Mountain flowers in color. London: Blandford Press. 428 pp.

Lense, Fritz. 1971. Naturschutz. München: Deutscher Alpenverein. (With 51 color drawings of protected plants plus a list of plants and animals protected in Bavaria, Germany.)

Tourist guidebooks

Austria and the Bavarian Alps. Michelin Green Guide. London: The Dickens Press. 218 pp.

Mountain Rambles in Austria. Austrian National Tourist Office. (Free from the office at 545 Fifth Avenue, New York, New York 10017.)

Internationaler Camping Führer. Band I, Südeuropa; Band II, Deutschland, Mittel- und Nordeuropa. ADAC Verlag GMBH, München. (Camping guides to southern Europe, Vol. I; and Germany and middle and north Europe, Vol. II.)

Climate
Kendrew, W.G. The Climates of the Continents. 4th ed. Oxford: Clarendon Press. 607 pp.

Glossary

Abdachung	gentle slope
Abfahrt der Züge	train departure (schedule)
Abhang	slope
Abkürzung	short cut
Abort	toilet, water closet
Absatz	platform, ledge
absteigen	to descend
Abstieg	descent
Absturz	cliff
abwärts	downward
Ache	river, stream
Alm	high mountain pasture
Alpe	high pasture
Alpenverein (AV)	Alpine Club
Ankunft der Züge	train arrival (schedule)
Ansicht	view
Ansichtskarte	picture postcard
aper	snow-free
aufsteigen	to ascend climb
Aufstieg	ascent
aufwärts	upward
Auskunft	information
Auslauf	outlet

Ausrüstung	outfit
Aussichtspunkt	viewpoint
Bach	brook
Bahnsteig	platform
Bahnverbindung	train connection
Band	shelf, ledge
befahrbar	passable
Berg	mountain
Bergführer	mountain guide
Berggasthof	mountain inn
Bergkrankheit	mountain sickness
Bergschrund	crevice separating glacier from rock
Bergsteiger	mountain climber
Bergsturz	rockslide
Bergwanderer	mountain hiker
Bett	bed
bewirtschaftet	open for business
bezeichnet (bez.)	marked
beziehungsweise (bzw.)	respectively
Blatt	sheet (map)
Bogen	bend
bratschig	broken in small pieces
breit	broad
Briefmarke	postage stamp
brüchig	broken, brittle
Brücke	bridge
Bühel, Bühl	hill, hillock
Decken	bedding; blankets

Dias	projection film slides
Dom	dome
Dorf	village
Drahtseil	wire rope or cable
draussen	outer (slope)
Einschnitt	notch
Einsenkung	saddle
Einstieg	start of climb
Eisbruch	ice-fall
Eisenbahn	railroad
empfehlen	recommend
empor	up, upwards
eng	narrow
entweder . . . oder	either . . . or
erforderlich	required
Ersteigung	ascent
Fahrweg	tertiary road
Fallinie	fall-line
Farbfilm	color film
Fels	upper rocky slope
Felsblock	boulder
felsig	rocky
Felsnase	rock spur
Felssporn	rock ledge
Felsturm	rock tower
Felswand	rock wall
Ferner	glacier
Fernsprecher	telephone
Firn	old corn snow

First	ridge
flach	flat
Flanke	flank
Flughafen	airport
Fluh	steep rock slope
Föhn	warm dry downslope wind; chinook
Führe	route
Führer	guidebook, guide
Furka (also, Fürkele, Furgga, Fürggele)	saddle or pass, generally with trail crossing
Fussweg	foot path
Gasthaus (also, Gasthof, Gaststätte)	inn
Gaststube	common room
Gebiet	region
Gebirge	mountain range
Gefahr	danger
gefährlich	dangerous
Gepäcksaufbewahrung	baggage checking room
Geröll	scree, rubble
Gesims	overhang, ledge
Gestein	rock
Gipfel	peak, summit
Gipfelkreuz	cross commonly found on peaks
glatt	smooth
Gleis	railroad track

Gletscher	glacier
Gletscherspalte	crevasse
Gletscherzunge	glacial tongue
Gondelbahn	gondola
Graben	ravine, trench
Grat	ridge
Gratturm	gendarme
Griff	grip
Grube	high nonforested cirque
Grübl	sink hole
Gruppe	mountain group
Güterseilbahn	cableway for transporting goods
Haken	peg
Halde	rubble from cliff, talus
Haltestelle	bus stop
Handtuch	hand towel
Hang	slope
Hangegletscher	hanging glacier
Hauptstrasse	main highway
Heilbad	hot springs
hoch	high
Höhe	height, summit
Höhenlinie	contour
höher	higher
Höhle	cave
Horn	horn
Hügel	hill or hillock
Hütte	mountain inn or hut

Hüttengebühren	hut fees or charges
Hüttenruhe ab 22 Uhr	quiet hours from 10 o'clock
jenseits	beyond
Joch	pass, ridge
Jugendherberge	youth hostel
Kabinenseilbahn	gondola lift
Kalkstein	"chalk stone"; limestone
Kamin	wide crack (in rock), chimney
Kamm	crest, ridge
Kante	edge
Kanzel	turret
Kapelle	chapel
Kar	glacial depression; cirque
Karboden	bottom of cirque
Karrenfeld	eroded limestone boulder field
Karrenweg	narrow cart track
Karte	map, card
Kaugummi	chewing gum
Kehre	curve, turn
Kessel	kettle
Kirche	church
Klamm	ravine, gorge
Kletterei	rock climb
klettern	to climb, scramble
Kloster	monastery
Kluft	crevice, gap, chasm

knapp	close, narrow
Kogel, Kofel	domed mountain
Kopf	head
Krummholz	low woody vegetation, usually above timberline
Kuppe	dome, rounded summit
kurz	short
Kurzführer	condensed guidebook
Landgrenze	boundary
Landkarte	map
Landschaft	landscape
Langspalte	longitudinal crevasse
Lawine	avalanche
Lebensmittel	provisions, foodstuffs
links	on the left
Leintücher	bed linen
lohnend	rewarding
mächtig	mighty
markiert	marked
Materialbahn	cableway for transporting goods
Matratzenlager	mattress-space, dormitory, sleeping loft
Mauer	wall, face
Möglichkeit	possibility
Moräne	moraine
morsch	rotten, breakable
Mulde	depression, hollow
nass	wet

Nebel	fog
Nebenstrasse	secondary road
Neigung	inclination, slope
nicht gestattet	"not permitted"
Nieder	lower, lesser
Nische	niche
Nord, Norden	north
Notlager	emergency sleeping accommodations
Notsignal	distress signal
nur für Geübte	only for experienced (hikers)
Oedland	barren land, as that above timberline
Ortsmitte	city center
Ost, Osten	east
Pächter	lessee, hut master
Pass	pass
Pfadspur	marked foot route
Pfeil	arrow
Pfeiler	buttress
Pickel	ice-axe
Platte	plateau
Postamt	post office
prächtig	splendid, magnificent
Quelle	spring, source
Quellmulde	boggy hollow
Quergang	cross-over, traverse
Querspalte	transverse crevasse

Randkluft	crevice between glacier and rock
rechts	on the right
Richtung	direction
ringsum	surrounding; round about
Rille	groove
Rinne	gulley
Rippe	rib
Riss	narrow crack (in rock)
Rücken	back
Rucksack	backpack
Rüfe, Rüfi, Rufi	rockslide
Sattel	saddle, pass
Scharte	notch, gap
Schichtung	layer
Schiefer	slate
Schigebiet	ski area
Schlafraum	dormitory
schliesslich	eventually, finally
Schlucht	ravine, gorge
schmal	narrow
Schnee	snow
Schrofen, Schroffen (also Schrotten)	partly wooded rocky mountain
schrofig	rocky and steep, often with a few trees
Schrund	crack, crevice
Schutt	rubble
Schutthalde	talus slope

Schutthange	talus slope at end of gully
Schuttkegel	debris cone
Schuttrinne	scree-filled gully
Schulter	shoulder
schwarz-weiss film	black & white film
Schwelle, Schwellung	mound, swell
schwierig	difficult
Schwierigkeit	difficulty
Schwindelfrei	free from dizziness; non-acrophobic
See	lake
Seil	rope
Seilbahn	cable car
Senke	depression
senkrecht	vertical
Sessellift	chair lift
Spalte	fissure, cleft; esp. glacial crevasse
Speisekarte	menu
Sperrmauer	dam
Spitze	peak, top
Sporn	spur
Spur	trail
Stafel	meadow barn or stall
Staudamm	dam
Stausee	reservoir, dam
Steg	narrow path or bridge
Steig	mountain trail
Steigeisen	crampons

Steiglein	minor trail
Steigspur	spur trail
steil	steep
Stein	stone
Steinmann	cairn
Steinschlag	rock avalanche
Strasse	street
Stufe	step, landing
Stunde (S. or St.)	hour (elapsed time)
Süd	south
sumpfig	swampy, boggy
Tal	valley
Talstation	valley station
Tauern	pass
Teich	pool, pond
Tobel, Tobl	ravine, often wooded
Törl	narrow pass; cleft
Träger	porter
Tritt	step
Trittsicherheit	sure-footedness
Trockenraum	drying room
über	via; over
Uebergang	crossing, bridge
Ufer	bank (of a river)
ü. M. or ü.d. M.	above sea level
Umgebung	vicinity
und so weiter (usw.)	and so forth
unerlässlich	indispensable
Unfall	accident, tragedy

Unterkunft	accommodations
Unterkunftshaus	tourist hut
Verbandszeug	first aid kit
vereist	glaciated
Verkehrsverein	tourist office
Vieh	cattle; stock
Vierzacker	four-point crampons
von . . . nach	from . . . to
von . . . zu	from . . . to
Vorgipfel	secondary summit
Vorsprung	rockledge, promontory
waagerecht	horizontal, level
Wald	forest, woods
Waldstreif	forest strip
Wand	mountain wall, face
Wanderweg	foot path
Wanne	depression; cirque, generally above treeline
Wasserfall	waterfall
Wasser sparen	"save water"
Wasserscheide	divide
WC	water closet, toilet
Weg	path, route
Weggabelung	fork (in a path)
weglos	without a trail
Wegtafel	trail sign
Wegteilung	trail fork
Wegweiser	trail sign

Weide	pasture
weiter	further
West, Westen	west
Wetter	weather
wichtig	important
Wiese	meadow
Wildbach	torrent
"Wirt"	hut manager
Wirtschafter	hut manager
Wirtshaus	inn, tavern
Wohnungsnachweis	tourist room list
Zahnradbahn	cog railway
Zelt	tent
Zeltplatz	camping place
Zickzack	zig-zag; switchbacks
Zimmernachweis	tourist room list

Acknowledgments

I wish to thank Dr. John Burbank for the photograph of Giglachsee appearing on page 105, and for checking the route descriptions in the vicinity of Ignaz-Mattis Hut. This is the only section I have not personally hiked.

My thanks go also to Professor Franz Fliri of the University of Innsbruck for assistance in collecting some of the weather data, and to François Mergen for checking my translation of the hut regulations.

−W.E.R.

About the Author

William E. Reifsnyder is Professor of Forest Meteorology and Public Health and chairman of the Interdisciplinary Program in Biometeorology at Yale University's School of Forestry and Environmental Studies. He is an inveterate hiker and backpacker, having rambled extensively in the High Sierra, the Rockies, the White and Adirondack mountains, Austria, and the Swiss Alps. Dr. Reifsnyder resides with his author-illustrator wife, Marylou, and their son, Gawain, in Middletown, Connecticut.

Field Notes

Field Notes

Field Notes

Field Notes

Field Notes

Field Notes

Field Notes

Field Notes

Field Notes

Field Notes

Field Notes